A Visionary MESSENGER

NOEL GRACE

BALBOA.PRESS
A DIVISION OF HAY HOUSE

Balboa Press books may be ordered through booksellers or by contacting:

Balboa Press
A Division of Hay House
1663 Liberty Drive
Bloomington, IN 47403
www.balboapress.com
1 (877) 407-4847

Because of the dynamic nature of the Internet, any web addresses or
links contained in this book may have changed since publication and
may no longer be valid. The views expressed in this work are solely those
of the author and do not necessarily reflect the views of the publisher,
and the publisher hereby disclaims any responsibility for them.

The author of this book does not dispense medical advice or prescribe the use
of any technique as a form of treatment for physical, emotional, or medical
problems without the advice of a physician, either directly or indirectly. The
intent of the author is only to offer information of a general nature to help
you in your quest for emotional and spiritual well-being. In the event you use
any of the information in this book for yourself, which is your constitutional
right, the author and the publisher assume no responsibility for your actions.

Any people depicted in stock imagery provided by Getty Images are
models, and such images are being used for illustrative purposes only.
Certain stock imagery © Getty Images.

Print information available on the last page.

ISBN: 978-1-9822-4442-2 (sc)
ISBN: 978-1-9822-4443-9 (e)

Balboa Press rev. date: 03/09/2020

CONTENTS

INTRODUCTION

Noel Grace, the author originates from the island of Jamaica, now retired and resides in the West Palm Beaches of Florida USA. He is the author and publisher of this and several other books including "Authenticity" & "Truly amazing Grace" Mr Grace specializes in the subjects of the human mind, the realities of life & the source of our existence. He continues to sound an alarm to awaken the human consciousness to identify and expidite their potentials.

Everything in existence with the exception of the elements of nature were conceived, materialized and implemented by way of the human mind. Our mind's capabilities cannot be exhausted but can be developed and utilized by doing adjustments to our mental paradigms. We are entering into an age of technology expansion and I encourage you to get on board for the ride and not get left behind.

None of the contents of this book is intended to be instructional, instead it's meant to be directive and motivational. Never allow the dark clouds of our today to impede the brilliant glow of a brighter future. Magnetize your being with knowledge to acquire and retain liquid substance, and be ascended to a higher elevation in existence. Invade the mental faculties of the mind in order to be creative.

Imagination is the innovative source of productivity and can be enormously rewarding. Have a wonderful life and enjoy it's pleasures. Enjoy the moments because every minute is a deduction from our allotted amount of time to live this life. Never try to make the impossible possible because everything happens for a reason, what is to be will be. There will be times when things happen and it would seem you were at the wrong place at the wrong time.

Let peace and love abide, cast your bread on the water and some day you will find it. Do not render evil for evil because compassion is of more value than retaliation. Our face impression, attitude and verbal utterances disclose our true mental contents, and our state of mind, curtail them. Each humen possesses 2 hearts, one an organ that circulates our blood and the other spiritual.

The mental heart is a processor located in a section of the brain adjacent to the minds and soul. Due to the lack of resource in the equation I will disclose that none of my books are edited. I'm just utilizing the natural potency of my intellect with elloquence. If at anytime you should encounter any errors due to my imperfection please disreguard them and proceed.

I will imply that the contents of all my publications are potent implications containing mental nutrients for conscious minds. I have been notified by my intellect that it's getting congested with mental substance to be disbursed to my international audience. The messege is clear and I will ensure that my assignment is accomplished by transparently disbursing it in this publication. I will endeavor to utilize adequate eloquence impacted with creativity.

My intent is to accomodate all my international audience of humanity worldwide, the only barrior is my inability to distrebute it in other languages presently.

Whenever we are going on a journey first thing we do is fill our gas tanks with fuel, likewise in our life pursuit we need God to be our security and protection from the evil adversary and his forces.

LET US PREY

Christ our Lord and Saviour, life and salvation, how excellent is your name throughout this earth. I come to you to ask for permission to approach the throne of grace by the only way to communicate with our father. Oh Father God Jehovah once more in spirit and in truth enhanced by the power of Holy your spirit.

We confess our short commings to you because we know you are mercyful, faithful and just to forgive us and cleanse us of all unrighteousness. Thank you for all our blessings, truth is light to our pathway to you and we give you thanks and praise Hallilujah.

Amen.

DEDICATION

I have dedicated my being to be an instrument of my maker to do his will for his purpose. It is benificial to enjoy every moment of our time as every minute is a deduction from our alloted amount of it to live this life. The preservation of our sanity is of vital importance to our existence, and the thoughts generated in the process should always be documented for the benefit of future generations.

Delete the concept of hoping from our vocabulary as it's like a gamble with high degree of uncertainties and stand secured in Christ. The two most powerful forces on this earth are nature and the human minds, the fact is they both are interveined by ignorance. My advise to all within my influence to seek and acquire wisdom through knowledge and from potent literature, because without knowledge the world will suffer. It's specified in the bible that the fear of God is the begining or wisdom, that's incorrect.

The acknowledgement of God as our main source that's where it's at, come taste and experience that the Lord is good and his mercies endures forever. There are no heavens out there in the atmosphere. The documentation that stated that the heavens declear the glory of God and the fermanent shows his handy works is misleading. God created a spiritual kingdom on a planet named heaven adjacent earth.

The earth rotates on a timer in the universe containing the world of humanity. It's my anticipation that the entire english world are deserning my indecations here. I do need a translator to help me get the words out there to benifit us all. Our saviour Jesus is not a Lord or God, he is a representative of God, Lord is a title of the trinity and God is also. There is no where in the bible where it says God uttered because he's invisible and do not utter.

Jesus was used as an instrument to vocalize God words followed by inspirations given by Holy his spirit to the contributers that wrote the bible. There are several other authors to this day including myself documenting the inspirations of god's words. Jesus said "I am the way truth and life, no one go to the father but by me" that was Christ the Word speaking through him.

Jesus was born a human by the vergin mary as a son of man long after the ark of Noah landed on dry ground, he was assigned the mission of doing the will of the father. The father was well pleased of his accomplishments so he beggotted/adopted him as a son, he's not a member of the trinity. I will declear to you that I'm just a messenger delivering one message thereby you will see me keep repeating the facts.

PREVIEW

Every human was made to be a component of this world with an allotment of time to accomplish a mission on planet earth. The question is...." What is your mission" No one knows specifically. The gaurantee is that some time in our life's pursuit we will do something significant to substantiate it. Always be on your guard to rezent the interventions of evil powers on your minds, errect a monument of progression. Use this treasure to nurture your piece of mind so it will glow like a fresh bloom in the dew of a brand new day.

None of the substance in this dialogue was designed to be delusional but all compiled to be practical. At this point in this exiciting adventure I am convinced that I was appointed to provide fuel for the fire of this venture as fertilizer to your minds. I am not in it for fortune or fame, all I need is evidence to convince me that my documentations have the effect intended on the world. The Word/Christ/Son is a component of God and assume the position of being a member of the trinity.

The trinity created the universe with all the planets including heaven, earth and everything in existence. The father held a conference with the Word/Christ and Holy his spirit, they decided to create the angelic forces of angels to occupy heaven with Michael the archangel as the head. They then created human in their likeness meaning three dimentional with their characteristics. They named them Adam and Lilleth, that's why the bible said male and female created he them.

The female was implanted with a portion of Adam's mentality which was not the way God planned it. The female was meant to be subjective so there had to be a correction, I will remind you that I am just a researcher. God chose the planet earth and put it in rotation on a timer to establish his kingdom on it, and devised a plan for it to be inhabited by humans and named it the world.

Another female was made from the dust of the earth and was named Eve, Adam's companion with a portion of his intellect. Lucifer was one of the angels in the angelic force and he defected to cause a short curcuit as a opponent to God. The first thing God hates is sin. he gave orders to be obeyed and one was violated by lucifer deceiving Eve. The maker did issue orders to put the process on hold. Eve disobeyed the rules of God and got deceived by the evil one creating the first sin. Eventually she had twin children, male and female when they were born she named the male Cain and the female Luluwah.

All other humans are made through the copulation process, Adam and Eve together had several other children as ordered to inhabit all parts of the earth. Adam and Eve eventually had a set of twins, and named the male Able and the female Acklia and she was more attractive. Time is of the essence but what better thing to do than caring for the unfortunate ones among us by nuturing their minds. We are approaching a uncomfortable zone here where it's emminent how precious we all are and the intricacies in the function of our being.

Based on my research I am convinced that each of us human beings have a timed blueprint designed by our maker and sustainer. The process was violated early in our existence by a sin called disobedience. There are times when a life is shortened by abusing our being, these abuses are manufactured by utilizing some of our senses to distroy our bodies. The main ones are feelings, taste and smell, these senses develop desires to be satisfied and eventually cause extingtion from life.

First I will welcome you in joining me in this dialogue and anticipate you consuming and comprehend the potency of the contents of it. It was not designed to be a religious book as I'm not a religious indevidual, although there are spiritual points to ponder it's an episcle by grace. We were all made three dimentional body, mind and spirit in the likeness of our maker and sustainer. I will admit that I am a child of Almighty God and a committed sheep of his pasture but not affilliated with any religion.

In the complecated field of literature the bible is catigorized as the word of God and a holy book, partially it's the only manual that substantiate our spiritually mental faculties concerning our existence and destinations. There are several versions of the bible and in different languages the most popular one is the King James version. Please do not get overwhelmed by me mentioning God as I am in the process of instilling in you, my readers vital information concerning our being.

Recently I had an extensive conversation with a young man concerning the realities of our being, there was another man in close proximity that listened my utterances. After the previous man left I was approached by the other man and he asked me what religion I was affiliated with and I told him none. I will remind you again that I am a researcher, last time I checked there are numerous religion even Jahovah's witnesses and church of Christ. Each religion has seperate beleafs. There's only one true God and only one way to approach him with prayers, thanks givings, suplications and praises.

My main source of spiritual resource is the bible because it's the only one that recorded history from before the beginning of time. Since I became an adult went through school, decided to pursue a career and made the decision to reseaserch the true source of my existence. I have read of incidences of individuals who chose to be religion ministers just like choosing any other career, some get wealthy. They have the habit of robbing the store house of the tithes and offerings people donate.

Ok let's get back to the root, after a long period of time all the children of Eve got to maturity and it became time for mating. Because the parents did not want them to interact with the partner they were born with they crossed them, so Able got the more attractive sister and it caused jelousy. Able became missing for days and it caused an alarm, eventually they found him dead, killed by his brother Cain who eventually ran off to the land of Nodd and found himself a wife

There are enormous amount of history of the past centuries concerning our ansesters and what transpired that affect our inheritance. Some with penalties but Jesus paid that price by the shedding of his redeeming blood.The bible contains enormouse amount of valuable instructions issued by God in three dimentions for us to comply by and give him honor and praise.

Lord is a title of God the trinity, God the father's name is Jehovah, to communicate with our father and maker in prayer we must do it in spirit and in truth, Christ is both, so we have access through him to our father. Jesus was never a spirit during the time he spent on earth, he had a spirit. After he accomllished his mission he was transformed and assended to heaven, he became a spirit when he received his reward and was begotted/adopted by the father as a son.

I was amazed to discover that all that time Lucifer had access to both heaven and earth. I am not a critic but I will discuss my observance of faulty spiritual practices concerning attemts of accessing the throne of Almighty God in the secret place of the most high. At this point in time christians who are perceived to be followers of Christ are praying in the name of Jesus, as devised by the evil adversary satan to prevent them from having access to the father who is not in heaven. There is only one way through Christ, I will remind you that to achieve our desire we must pray in spirit and truth.

I will also advise my catholic friends to go through Christ also and not Mary. I hope you are still here with me, basically what I'm doing here is to brighten your pathway to reality. It's not my intent to overwhelm you with this information, I discovered in my recearch so you have the right to investigate it for yourself also. I'll tell you there is only one truth and it's Christ now under attack. It's of vital importance that we develop the habbit of reading potent literature and medetate on the things of God.

Do not allow your vital privilages to be diverted by the evil one, presently his main instrument is the social media and TV. Our spirtuality is essential to explore and comply with the requirements according to the will of God. There is only one truth and it's useless to debate that fact as there are no alternatives. Relgions are diversive and misleading based on the interpretations people comprehend from the bible. In most cases there are documentations that are literal and devisive. It is unusual for the preview of a book to be this extensive but it's beneficial to prepare for the main event.

It's specified in the bible that God hates sin, devorces and sexual immorality. There came a time in the previous world when sin became rampant poluting the will of God. Recently there was a massive demonstration of homosexuals in the US and there were several religous involved. The pope head of the catholic religion recently declear that homosuality is legal. The eveil adversary is buisy in the process of enlarging his domain, we have to be on our guard and rely on the father through Christ to chase satan to flee from us his people.

The earth was cleansed through a process designed by God, Noah was one of Adam's off spring and God used him to build a boat, load it with his family and numerous other living things in preparation for the process. One day rain started falling emencely causing a total flood of the earth destroying the entire first world, there is a new world ordered.You and I are components of the new cleansed world and decendants of Noah. My advice to you is to put on your mental armor of consciousness in preparation for the duration of your lifetime.

There will be other generations before the end of time, and there will be another cleansing by fire before the eternal kingdom comes with everlasting life in paradise. This is all based on the decesions we make. You may get curious and ask if I'm not into religion how do I give honor, thanks and praise to our father. My advice to you is to submit your being by accepting Jesus and establish a personal relationship with the father by way of Christ. Please enjoy the pleasure of me sharing my insperations with you.

Please endeavor to read the complete book, you will be glad you did and be fully educated to prepare for enjoying paradise. We are approaching an unconfortable area of our encounter, to instill in you the realities of your lives I will apologise for taking you outside the comfort zone, please prepare your being for this mental voyage.There will be times in this dialogue when things will seem ambigeous, don't ask me to clarify as I'm only a messenger. Every moving object doe's require a source to propel it and in the case of us authors our source cannot be interrogated.

My primary challenge for you is to read this book in it's entirety and try to identify my main motive to preserve the being of humanity to prevail. I am making an appeal to all humanity to read more to acquire knowledge and from knowledge you will derive wisdom. Wisdom is fuel for our brain so our positive thoughts issue directives for us to progress. Since I commenced my research I am discovering that capabilities of the potency of our being is under utilized. That's the reason I am convinced that there will be other generations after ours.

There are possibilities to be discovered to benifit human existence. The most recent evidence of my research is the pace of the expansion of technology, there are more to come from it. Presently technology is in the process of setting up the infrstructure for the next extensive trend on our way to infinity. At this point in existence I will imply that the educational system discontinue focusing on the subject history as it's the past and consentrate on preparing for the future.

History is of the past which comes not back, there is no reverse in our life's transmission. We are either in forward or park, the latter implies retardation. Let's get back to our local environment, there are sections of our vocabulary that is inadiquately utilized and one is called common sense. It's dangerous identifying a lion as a sheep, it is not wise to substitute sugar with salt and where there's smoke there's fire. Another is saving the best for last, in most cases the laws of sequence are violated to benifit reality.

Realities do have alternatives and that's when right choices complicate the process in order to achieve positive benifits. Life is a timely predestined journey that's uniquely designed specifically for each individual. There are times when we do assessments of ours and do a comparison to someone else's and realize that there are always people who are going through worse situations. I do not know either of my parents as they passed when I was too young, I do have a picture of my father and saw one of my mother once.

Thats why I rezent seeing children dislike, disrespect, desert, neglect and abuse their parents. I can imagine how sweet and pleasurable it is to hear your mom say I love you with a kiss. In my entire life I have never had a physical fight, I've had verbal disagreements but always walk away in the shadow of a doubt. It's very important to keep our emotions under control, there are times when the situation is over we realize it was a waisted effort. Selfcontrol and patience work together, you cannot have one without the other.

FOOD FOR THE MIND

We must make a commitment as to where we'll be for eternity, always give respect and recognition to Almighty God Jehovah who sustains us and he will direct our pathway. I will declear that I am a child of God and a sheep of his pasture but not involved in religions as they are devisive, I have a personal relationship to communicate with the father by way of Christ his son. I make it a routine to medidate on his laws day and night and awaits my compensation package.

We are all capable to utilize the potent products of our minds, we need to hold on to the hands of our sustainer. God is a spirit and we all must worship him in spirit and in truth through Christ. He is invisible but can be discerned. Our beings are monitored and sustained from inception the final destinatination we choose. Wisdom is derived from knowledge which comes from literature and understanding is the nutrient. A wise man is empowered by knowledge and has the capability to convey and distribute it.

All planets and the fullness thereof were created by God and we are components of the world and interact with other elements to cause an impact on our existence. A farmer experiments with vegetation and produces food and the human brain does have the capability of discernment which is essential. There are instructions left for us by our maker to direct our pathway. It was disclosed that we should seek first to attain the previlage to acquire access to the kingdom of God and all things will fall in place.

I will encourage the young ones among us to get attached and learn from us adults experiences as experience teaches wisdom. The subconscious mind work in conjunction with the will to determine actions to be taken based on the information acquired from the senses. The conscious mind does the execution and command the actions to be taken to accomplish the end product. Never allow yourselves to be distracted based on deceptions, there are negative consequences for any errors.

God the father does have a name and his name is Jehovah, he is omnipotent and omnipresent and although his spirit is invisible he can be spiritually discerned. Insist on making each day of life a difference, never allow your lives to become a routine. There are times in the pursuit of life when it would seem like we are involved in a competition, but life is not a gamble it is a privilege. Each day is unique and you will never see it again, make the best of it. No one can turn back the hands of time, so we all should get on the ride for the duration of our alotted time.

A thought is a perceptive product generated by the conscious mind, depending on the motive at origination, can be highly productive or destructive. Of all the systems involved in the duration of the human's life, the thinking process is the most imperative. The quality of our thoughts determines our full potential. I will encourage everyone to get involved in the farming of your minds. Cultivating productive thoughts for the benefit of the next generation.

The human conscious mind is basically a processor of information to cause an impact. One of the greatest products of mind power is the invention of technology and the pace of it's impact on civilization. Most or about all systems are controlled by computers but relies on human directives as to the limits and timing of it's functions. There are no restrictions as a limits to the utilization of acquired knowledge. Destiny is a reality and the blueprint of our being.

There are diversions caused by the evil forces but they can only intercept your mind based on your vulnerability. The human mind set is crucial based on the potency of our intellect, deception is inevitable. Two of the most important actions of life are the decisions and choices we make, they are the traffic lights of life. If for any reason we make an error in any of them there are consequences to encounter. If you make the right ones you will reap the benefits and if you make bad ones you suffer the consequences.

As we go along here you will realize the mention of God as he is the source of our being, if for any reason you are not a God fearing person feel free to skip those pages. In all systems there have to be coordination of the components involved. In the process of human existence we have the father Jehovah, Christ the son and the power of Holy his spirit. We were made in God's likeness so we have a body, a soul and a spirit. These are all components of our being.

Whoever is spiritually conscious to comprehend the whole aspects of our existence will eventually comply with the requirements in order to attaining the gift of everlasting life. The human life is basically a culmination of several systems operating in sequence to complete a process. In most cases habits and lifestyles impede it to cause complications. For example smoking is a critically destructive habit that cause several organs to malfunction and people do it.

Sickness is caused by the malfunctioning of certain organs that initiate the deterioration of life. Doctors have discovered ways by using various medicines to curtail them. Presently there is a multimillion dollar chemical warfare industry against the eminent death. Life was given to us to live it eternally but if we allow ourselves to be diverted by deceptions. The second heart is an invisible asset located in the brain and is the true you when materialized in words and actions.

Love, compassion, conscience, affection and generosity are just a few of the products of the mental heart. Both the minds and the mental heart are neighbors in the brain. They are maintained by the piece of God that preserves all understanding. I will make no appology reminding you that God is in full control of our destiny at all times as he made all things and is the source of existence.

The information superhiway is moving at a rapid pace and it is still amazing that the turbulence of aero aviation does not disturb it. The human mind have different folders and they all work together to develop innovations to perpetuate civilization. It is healthy to daydream, using your imagination to generate productive thoughts. America sent austronauts to check the possibility of other living creatures and found nothing. We humans occupy this earth and on planet heaven there are the angelic host just as God planned it.

At this initial stage of this venture my main intent is to awake the human mental consciouness as to the realities of life. Based on the nature of the contents of this book it will arrive at a time when it's difficult to be catigorized. The bible is catigorized as being the spiritually holy words of God. Spirituality is the main foundation of excellence of our existence from creation. There are several others and I'll analize them as we go along here.

I am a researcher and my main sources of vital information are derived from documentations and literature with potent substance. My main objective is to share my findings with you and in no way trying to indoctrinate you like religions do. Certainly you will not agree with all my views but we must tolerate eachother perceptions. The next essential element in our existence is equelibrium, that means balance and we all vitally need that even to maintain a vertical position.

Yesterday I had to go to the Dr and ended up parking on the eighth floor parking lot looking at the skyline. This was downtown Miami Florida USA and I looked to the east at the highrise buildings and was astonished in amazement as to how they remain vertical. Eventually I regained consciousness and realized that in order for them to go up and stay there, they had to build an infrastructure underground. We are at a critical area of existence and I am not careful you will question if my mental stability is in place.

Another aspect of our being is resource also known as energy, the resource for momentom relies on some kind of it in three forms. Liquid solid or monitary, we could say like putting fuel in the fire. There are several aspects of it like industrial, transportation the stock market and medical field, there are humans also running on electriticy. There is also an industry called insurance that are contributed to and pay the final bills.

It's our responsability to utilize our five senses effectively to supply substance for our brain to function efficiently. So as not to get you bored another is our minds, we are a very complecated entity but is capable of being who we are as designed by our maker. There are others but I short changed you as I did not elaborate enough on the substances involved.The dreams we get in our sleep is the subconscious mind working overtime with delusions from the evil forces.

Never discuss or share your dreams with anyone because the negative forces can intercept and prevent them from materializing. The PC is one of the greatest inventions created by man, and contributes to most of the aspects I mentioned earlier. It is loaded with memory and processing power but lacking of intelligence so relies on human directives to achieve and produce products to impact civilization and beyond.

This again displays the potency of the human conscious mind as whatever it perceives can be achieved and enhanced by technology. My cellular phone acts also as a computer, I am able to do just about anything on it. Recently I saw a lady on the internet on my phone and asked her for her location and she told me she was in Australia, that's amazing. I did mention our options of making choices in this life, seek redemption in accepting Jesus our saviour and the Holy the spirit of God in our hearts.

Loosing our soul is the greatest loss ever, it's much more benificial to acquire everlasting life with Christ as designed for us by our father. I will inform you that I have a very curious mind and is always doing explorations to verify realities. Recently I wondered how old is this earth presently we are living in the year 2020 and the only book that contain such old record is the bible. My perception is that there were generations before us and more to come.

It is the responsibility of parents to direct children in the adoration of God and anticipate that when they grow up they will not depart from it. It's benificial to have them interacting with nature and monitor the friends they associate with. It's unfortinate that spiritually religious leaders instill false hope in human minds, like when someone dies they go to heaven and walk the streets of glory. The only transformed human that's been to heaven is Jesus and there will be on one else.

Recently I had the opportunity to baby sit my six years old grand daughter and we had the privilege to communicate. This is something I always do to investigate a child's chain of thought, so I asked her what kind of work her mom and dad does and she specifically told me. Moving right along I asked her what will she do when she grows up to be an adult. In most cases it's an ambiguous venture because they are in a confused state of mind.

To my amazement she said she wants to be a thinker that read books, I was truly amazed. Our children are the next generation and there have to be of all different skills and professions. It is benificial for kids to grow up in a family environment although I did not have the previlage of it, I grew up as an orphan at an early age as both of my parents died early. One of the most potent asset we possess is our mind and consiousness, it is what seperate us from other living creatures.

It is our responsibility to allow it to be adjusted and colabered by some instructions mentioned in the bible. Our conscience is similar to a compass that directs a ship or plaine. It is of vital importance that we allow God's recipe to guide us on the right pathway to eternal life. Satan and his evil forces attack our minds even in our sleep to divert our minds to the state that when we leave this life off track he can claim us to accompany him to distruction in that lake of fire, instead of awaiting resurection to go to paradise.

As the bible state, it is easier for a cammel to go through the eye of a needle than for a rich man to enter the kingdom of God. I will confess that although a book can earn me resource, it is not my intention to gain any amount of substantial gain. My main intent is to get the minds of the world aware and activated to participate in the process of expanding the kingdom of God. The instructions given was to go out into all the world preaching the words of God, so other humans will accept Jesus by grace.

Get submerge in water as his redeeming blood in the names of the father, Christ his son and Holy his spirit. I will caution you that if you see anything mentioned here more than once it is not deliberate but beneficial because repetition is the adesive that attaches information to the memory folder of the conscious mind. It is substantially rewarding to magnetize the mechanism of the intellect in order to absorb the necessary information, for the development process.

There is a ladder for success and we must seek and derive the necessary requirements in the pursuit of life. It is easier to descend than ascend, every step represents an elevation and they all are attainable. Regardless of where you are on the ladder never look back to be distracted or reminded of the past. Life is a one time journey with an allotment of time to accomplish a mission. It is important to identify your niche and utilize your potentials to achieve the ultimate goal.

There will be an end to time, what matters between now and then is not the distance but what we accomplish in the duration. It's a good practice to emulate the principles of the insignificant ants by storing up substance for rainy days and utilize the power of unity. There are components of the human being that are indestructible and will exist forever based on our decisions. The two most powerful components are our will and soul they are the ultimate authority.

I will encourage you to research and make a determination as to the destiny of our being in the next phase of life. The decisions we make do have consequences and it is of paramount importance that we analyze our thoughts before acting. It is like having two coins in a fountain and have to choose which to acquire. Our actions are continuously monitored and there will be compensation based on the polarity of the effects of our deeds, negative or positive.

This is vital information and the opposing forces do not want this to be exposed to retard their agenda. The mortal components of each human being is on a timer and will eventually end based on the appointment with death. There are destinations issue and we have to decide our destiny before we die. The information you are being exposed to here is very potent and because of the divisive programs set up by the adversary most people miss out.

Each human was uniquely made a self-contained entity with enormous amount of mental assets and capabilities to make decisions. The problem is, because of distractions and deceptions most of them are inadequately utilized.This is a wake-up call for the masses to wake up and get with the program. The intent of my mission is to take you to the bridge for you to seek information as to our purpose in order for you to take the plunge.

My hope is that you will discern the vision in the content of this endeavor so our thought process is reformed to culminate the journey successfully. Literature is the life blood of mental empowerment and knowledge like blood is to the mortal body. It is more beneficial to read a good book at leisure than watch the television.The electronic media serves two purposes, information and entertainment. Never allow yourselves to become vulnerable so you are controlled by the agents of deceptions.

Currency in adequate moderation is the life blood of survival, seek and devise legal means to open doors to access and enjoy the benefits of it. All humans were uniquely made and collectively named the world and placed on the planet earth to accomplish individual assignments. There are no two completely identical humans. Partnerships are beneficial and productive but it is difficult to coordinate it based on the differences in opinions, thoughts, ideas and demeanor.

Never allow your emotions to disturb the bloom of your demeanor, control it. The impression on your faces including the teeth exposes your state of mind.There are three realms that we have to encounter in our tremendous journey, the mortal, the spiritual and eternal for who make it there. We were born and given the choice to make a decision as to the final destination of our being.

The natural is not everlasting but timed and when it is over where we go depends on the choice we made.

The fact is this, if we do not make one it will be made for us and we'll be claimed by satan the evil one. These are realities of life, the routine devised by satan is to have us concentrate on his trivial agenda and miss out. There is a simple process of redemption by accepting the free gift given to us based on the ransom paid by the sacrificing of Jesus. I hope you are paying attention to the information I am disclosing here to your benefit to end up on the good side in the spiritual realm.

Happiness will keep us sweet, trials will keep us strong, challenges will keep us human and success will keep us growing. The most essential word is confidence it is best to trust it, always acquire the facts and equipt yourselves with certainty. Always enhance your demeaner with a smile, it project your state of mind and help to brighten the day. Each time I go to use the restroom I have the tendency to sing and shout for joy, it says in the word that we should come before his presence with singing.

With knowledge oh taste and see that the Lord is good and his goodness endures forever. The writing of this book is an assignment given to me to accomplish a mission. Being an author is sometimes straineous on the brain but over time you develop the technicalities to sustain consciousness. Satan is a name you will not see much in this dialogue as I was instructed to resist and rezent him and he will flee from me.

To mention his name is a mean of promoting his agenda and that is like putting a car in reverse. Recently I was aproached by a family member of mine but one of his agents and was told to discontinue writing these kinds of books. I did rezent that encounter and continued doing the will of my father, this is an asignment. I was recently approached by an agent of a publishing company and he insisted on selling me an expensive promotional packege.

The thing is at this late point of my life I am not seeking fortune or fame. I dedicated my being to be utilized by my maker to expand his kingdom by ways of the mental hearts of humanity. Seasons will come and go but the aquisition of a pass to paradise is eternal. Insperations by way of meditation is essential as it attracts the attention of conscious minds. God is our maker and sustainer and due to the distractions caused by the evil adversary, vulnorable minds are gone astray.

I'm being used to devise means to bring them back home to expand the kingdom here on earth. With open arms Jesus will accept anyone that is willing to repent and return to the right pathway to paradise. Soft words have been spoken and hearts have been broken, do not allow yourself to be a victim of the past. Each day is a present and a new step on the ladder of life. Be persistent and endure the obsticles you encounter along the way.

Continually give thanks to our sustainer for our blessings and the beauty of nature that surround us with rose petals, the sounds of the sparrows and the churp of the nightengales. Regardless of the cloudy skies in my rural neighborhood, may the joy of the Lord today make your anticipations brighter. My assignment is to promote the formula to acquire eternal life utilizing potent literature to make life worth living. We were all made in the likeness of God in three dimentions consisting of a body, soul with a spirit expanded to consist of love with affection.

It is of vital importance that we first love our maker then ourselves and our neighbors as ourselves. As it's specified in the bible that all human have an appointment with death and after death there will be a judgement for wrong deeds. My hope is that mejoriety of us make the right choices in order to inherit paradise. In the pursuit of life I tried to acquire as much education as I could and got to high school, my regret is not being able to speak any other language but english.

My desire is to reach out to all the world to enhance them with the information needed to head in the right direction. As an author my intent is to magnitize the contents of my publications so people will hunger hungry for more. The minds of the masses are being distracted based on the deterorating trends of this system of things devised by the evil adversary. Be cautious, seek and acquire potent substance to empower your minds with knowledge as from knowledge comes wisdom.

It's more benificial to be a victor than being a victim of circumstance and be vulnoreble to negativity. It's becoming more challenging, you must equipt yourselves to counteract the negative trends to be successful. Again I will reinterate that if you should see anything mentioned more than once it's not intentional but benificial as repetition promotes retention. Our human minds are the root of mortal existence and the most potent asset we possess.

My best friend is my celular phone and I named him Donald, he retains eighty percent of my secrets and priveracy. He contain a bible, a dictionary and my contact list. It has a calculator and much more to mention, I'm at the point where sometimes for days I don't turn on my desktop PC as I am storing substance for my books in it. Being an author there are times when I am out and around and substances comes in my mind and instead of using a note pad there's Donald.

Another area of life that is critical is the overhaul maintenance consisting of absorbtion, disposal of waste, health, hygiene and exercise. Our external presentation is of vital importance also for both genders, this department created an expensive industry for the ladies. The hair, nails, fragrances, makeup, and jewelry is a mulitmillion dollors industrial complex. Whereby on the other hand all we men require is a fresh haircut, dump, shave and shower, a classy suit, shoes and a cologne with lasting residual, the car keys and off we go.

I consider being a medical doctor a complicated profession as there are no two identical human. One of the most complicated aspects of our being is our brain, located in our head that's where the main control center is located. Our brain require and obtain vital information from our senses and most of them are located on the same limb, the head. The information the brain gets is processed by our subconscious mind then sent to the conscious mind to be executed.

That's why it is not safe to make decisions in a rush as it have to be pondered by our mental heart. In this life democracy is very important whereby we have alternatives to resort to, my appointment with reality is to gaurantee our satisfaction in this endeavor. Here we get back on track, there is an ultematum called abuse in the equation and bad habbits is one of them. Habbits is an abusive trend, humans indulge in them and exit life before living it.

Alcohol, tobacco, coffee and other illegal drugs are distructive to the mortal structures and people allow thomselves to become addictive to them. Because of the fragile foundation on which the system of things is built vulnorable human minds lost it's capability to comprehend and concentrate on the complexity of existence. God our maker and sustainer is systemitic as to the processes he set in place for the perpetuation of our being.

I was amazed seing a mother delivered ten female and one male children. Presently I'm in the process of utilizing the principles I've learnt and is anticipating having two best selling books for activating minds for the twenty first century.With God all things are possible, he is the one feeding my mental faculties with potent substance from inspirations to share with you all. Do not allow yourselves to be detered from being compassionate, it's a blessing to tell others God bless them and you love them.

Ever since I was a youngster I always had an older friend, I always learn from their experiences they share with me. There is a saying that says iron sharpens iron, here I am trying to awake your awareness so you wake from your slumber. Always be carefull of what you feed your mind with, you cannot plant corn and reap pease.The thought process is vitally important to utilize positively for the purpose of enlightening our knowledge to tolerate the realities of life and survive.

A close associate of mine confieded in me to tell me that he does not beleave in God, that is sad and I was disappointed to hear him say that. I further discovered he was going through a phase, we all go through them but the lack of knowledge of the truth is like fuel to the fire. Patients is a virtue that lighten the mental overload on our minds, in most cases the things we worry about work themselves out eventually. I will not take credit for being a very patient person of coarse I have become a lot more tollerant since I am getting up in age.

There were times in my younger days when all my patients were in the hospital. There are some very impatient people around and sometimes they cause confrontations, like people that like to cut lines. I witnessed sometime ago in a parking lot where a man was sitting quite patiently in his car waiting for someone to exit a space so he could park his car. A car left and in went this lady from no where, disregarding the waiting man. Of course that caused a major disturbance with exchanges of strong verbal language, it is very hurtful when people do those things.

It is important to realize that we all live in an environment controlled by time so we have to make the necessary adjustments and consider others. There are also incedents while driving on the roads, I was waiting at a light and the light changed but the car ahead of me did not move so I toot my horn and it moved. The same thing reoccured at the next light, I try to practice what I preach. At the third light I was beside the car and discovered it was a female putting on her makeup.

This is becoming common practice in the mornings and sometimes it cause people to loose their kool. In life we allow yourselves to be cought up in the sideshow and miss out on the main event. We get buisy in the pursuit of happiness and forget to be happy. Buisy making a living and forgot to live. It is very benificial to practice tollerance, compassion, affection and meekness as it's predicted that the meek ones will inherit paradice on the new and cleansed earth.

I discovered my ability to be an author when I turned sixty and it's amazing the amount of substance I receive to process and impart to my readers. I will say there are certain realities we have to acknowledge, truth also known as fact are absolute and is inconsequential to debate or dispute. The other is the origination of all things under the universe including you and I. This is not a religous book although there are spiritul contents injected in the dialogue.

Regardless of our persuation I encourage you to read the complete book timely and with an open mind. Be aware that success is attainable with mental aspirations in conjunction with adjustments to the parameters of our mental paradigms. One man's fear is another man's fortune, always aim for the gold if you should acquire the bronze it is better than nothing. I was appointed to distribute this vision so whoever is exposed to it will utilize it for their benifit.

VISIONS

200 Gems to enhance your lives and cause happiness.

*T*he following are original quotes devised by the author in an effort to energize our awareness as to the capabilities of the conscious mind if utilized wisely. Have a wonderful and eventful life and do enjoy our privileges.

1. The success of our lives rely on the quality of our thoughts; invest in the coordination of our mental faculties.

2. Life is a privileged venture with an allotment of time to fulfill a mission.

3. Live, love and give to be blessed and compensated by the main source.

4. Our value is not determined by our material possessions but by our deeds. Start laying up treasures in deeds to be compensated.

5. It is pleasurable to indulge in meditation with the sound of the nightingales chirping sweet melodies on the distant horizons.

6. Revitalize our mental consciousness and generate aspirations to pursue and acquire a successful outcome.

7. It is productive to engage in mind farming, it creates innovations for products to benefit our existence.

8. Respect the views and opinions of others even if you disagree and do not expect them to accept yours.

9. To ignore is a choice but to be ignorant is a defect, seek knowledge, it's kinetic energy, power and might.

10. Every human's life is controlled by a thought process, take actions to keep it in forward and not reverse.

11. There would be a void in life without the challenges, there is always a light beyond the tunnel.

12. Endure the circumstances we encounter to the best of our ability, at the end of the rainbow there will be a pot of gold.

13. When the night falls it is time for our faculties to rest and recuperate for the dawning of a new day. It is productive to have dreams.

14. It is important to synchronize our being with time for accurate functioning; there is a time and place for everything.

15. Differentiate our wants from our needs, wants are fueled by desires and needs are essentials for survival.

16. All humans are three dimensional, in conference God who is three dimensional in nature but is individual in function, decided to make human in his charistical likeness.

17. If you allow ignorance to supersede knowledge, a vacuum called vulnerability is created to accommodate negativity.

18. Surprises sure make life exciting; do not rely on anyone to surprise you. Invest in yourselves within your means.

19. Stress is a defective bi-product of defective decisions, indulging in stress is a recipe for exiting life on the stress express prematurely.

20. The term world is the total count of all human beings. The earth is a created domain we occupy temporarily.

21. It is pleasurably rewarding to be successful, but the secret of survival is not to be selfish, seek means to give and satisfy needs.

22. Sow seeds of compassion and some day in the future it will bear a fruit as compensation.

23. Because the man devised system have recreated human in a negative mode to sustain it, the default has become the normal, resent it.

24. Let us all cherish this day and give thanks to the main source, there is no guarantee we will see tomorrow.

25. Keep our concentrations focused on the good things in life and aspire elevating to high horizons.

26. Every human being is a self contained power plant with enormous amount of capabilities.

27. Respect and analyze the power of the spoken word before you utter, once it is disbursed it cannot be retracted. Listen more and talk less.

28. The key to abundance is the practice of sharing our prosperity, it is better to give than receive.

29. Everyone feed their body at least three times a day; it is of vital importance that we feed our minds with potent nutrients constantly.

30. Make sure our affirmations are synchronized with our determination in order to achieve our goals.

31. There is a demand for negative content due to the trends of time, you are never alone God is always with you,

32. The reason men get bald in the head is because that's where the antenna for the brain is. If a man is totally bald does not mean he is smarter.

33. The human conscious mind is the absolute authority of his existence, it validates information from the senses and determines actions to be taken.

34. Common sense enhances the level of intelligence, to be smart and lacking of common sense is dangerous.

35. Every human have an appointment at different stages with different deaths. It is important to seek knowledge and prepare for it.

36. Seek positive programming of the minds to counteract the earth system of things. Seek the Lord while he can be found and call upon him while he is near. It is important to prepare for landing on the new earth when resurected.

37. Carefully explore the fields before you join the herd, the grass always seem greener on the other side until you get there.

38. Let us all pursue the journey of life exploring the realities of our existence and prepare to endure the circumstances for the duration.

39. Color is used to determine the degree of bad and is divisive. The darkest color is black and all other colors are derived from it except white. White is not a color or is it pure, it's a neutral pigment that can be manipulated to create other colors.

40. It would be good and pleasant for everyone to live in peace, love and unity. The outcome would be like honey dripping from a honeycomb empowered with sweetness.

41. Every human's life is on a blueprint with a magnetic force guiding it from inception to extinction.

42. I have no authority and none of this content is instructional, this material is an assignment with substance filtering through my intellect.

43. As long as something is included in our anticipation to achieve, never use the word if, substitute it with when in order to have a positive outcome.

44. There is evidence that the law of attraction is operating in a reverse mode because the negatives are becoming the norm. History usually repeat itself and have consequences.

45. Vacuum is created by empowering emptiness, always be careful of our situation because our senses operate in a state of vacuum.

46. Cherish whatever you possess and seek ways to improve it, it is better to have a live mouse than a dead lion.

47. There is no perfection in civilization, vulnerability complicates outcomes and creates consequences.

48. Hello world! Always realize that time is fuel; utilize it to the maximum before it runs out.

49. The world inhabits the earth; we all are one connected by air as long as we are breathing and it's poluted, vegetation included.

50. It is more expensive to be ignorant than educated, in ignorance we make expensive blunders and suffer the consequences.

51. Before you can make anyone happy you have to make ourselves happy first, material things does not necessarily make someone happy.

52. Identify and maintain our brand, do not try to emulate others. Every human was made uniquely equipped to create and survive the duration from inception to extinction.

53. Practice sowing seeds of compassion and blessings on a regular basis to generate rewards in our compensation account.

54. Hope and fear are relevant but not related, lonelyness is not a reality, it is productive to find someone to relate to in confedence.

55. Always have an open mind. The human mind is like a parachute, it operates better when it's open.

56. Cross the river of circumstances, aim for the mountain of prosperity and overlook the valleys of adverseties.

57. Always call a friend and tell them you thought of them, it is always good to be eachother's keeper.

58. Always give thanks to our main source of life, as today is the beginning of the rest of our existence.

59. Curtailment retards progress let freedom reign and humanity continue to advance on this revolving planet.

60. If life was a song how often would you sing it? Utilize all our abilities to the fullest and enjoy it's pleasures.

61. Hoarding is a selfish game and giving creates a magnet to attract abundance.

62. It is always better to the best of our ability to be our true self than to be discovered to be someone else.

63. Having everything will not necessarily make you happy, making the best of what you have will.

64. It is possible to do something in an instant that causes you pain for a lifetime.

65. There will be times in life that circumstances causes us pain; it does not give us the right to be cruel.

66. The accurate execution of the power of the human will, determines the final destination of the soul.

67. As the dew on the leaves greet the sunlight of a new day, so should you welcome the privileges and maximize their potentials.

68. The people with the most money did not work to acquire it, quite the opposite. They had money work for them to achieve it.

69. Hope is a doubtful state of anticipation; we must take positive actions to achieve our goals.

70. As a nation in all our undertakings we must cling to the best until better comes. Without vision a people will perish.

71. The progress of a nation relies on the choices of it's people, let us all cling to the gold standard.

72. The compensation system is alive and well, be alert to identify your blessings as sometimes it comes disguised.

73. The sun does not come up nor the moon go down, the planet earth that we inhabit revolves around them.

74. Always be conscious of the indoctrinations in the diversion from the truth and guard your minds not to be devoured.

75. Expand your horizons and extend a helping hand to help the under privileged.

76. Liquid is a vital state of existence; never allow our being to become stagnant.

77. This journey of life is a one way trip, with a mission to accomplish, endeavor to make an impact on society.

78. The prefix tech is a platform and a road map for advancement, get on board and not get left behind.

79. There are only two words in the English language that have all five vowels in order "abstemious" and "facetious".

80. Currency is the life and blood of commerce, we must devise legal means of acquiring, utilize and retaining it.

81. Try to live a life of purpose with all our faculties in a positive and sequential motion to cause an impact on society.

82. All is said and done, destiny is predestined although we can be at the wrong place at the right time.

83. Look-up, in the atmosphere to behold the glory of the Almighty God and prepare our intellect to accept inspirations.

84. The world with all it's mortal inhabitants in a package called time is temporary on this planet earth. Our souls can live everlasting in paradise based on a single decision.

85. The state of total tranquility called piece is a state of mind and is the preservative for our heart and mind. Let no one disturb them.

86. Jehovah God created one male, the rest of us were born by a process, we must acquire wisdom from knowledge for survival.

87. The ultimate heights of spiritual greatness will not be attained by sudden flight, but by utilizing capabilities of our thoughts while others sleep.

88. The English language has 26 letters and this sentence uses all 26... "The quick brown fox jumps over the lazy dog"

89. The challenges in life's pursuit retard the true purpose of living life to the fullest, but we can conquer it.

90. Mentally it is productive to have a song in our hearts at all times, but not the one that says." I am myself and no one else".

91. "Dreamt" is the only word in the English language that ends with the letters mt, it is benificial to dream.

92. It is a proven fact, that mystery, fiction, delusion and material with evil contents are devised to attract more interest than reality.

93. The fastest growing belief system on earth is a wagon going in the wrong direction to destruction called Islam. We must guard our minds from it.

94. The human conscious mind have the capability of accomplishing anything that's perceived.

95. The process of repetition is the means by which information gets attached to our minds.

96. Allow yourselves to be in environments to feast on the magnificence of nature. The fragrance of roses, the chirping of birds and the wind.

97. A live human is plural in nature and never alone or stationary, even while sleeping.

98. A positive thought is a mental seed awaiting germination to substantiate it's existence.

99. The human body is a self contained power plant with enormous amount of potentials to develop and impact existence.

100. Live well and laugh often, as laughter is therapy for the soul, and love a lot. Make the best of now like there is no tomorrow.

101. Never give up on the pursuit of our dreams as they were our hopes of yesterday to be achieved and accomplished.

102. Happiness is a generated state of mind, seek means of perpetuating the benifits of it when it's acquired.

103. Devise means to derive resource and strive to survive, always put God first then yourselves and do not exceed the limits.

104. Our determinations specifies the intent of what we perseive to achieve, enjoy it's blessings and give thanks to the Almighty.

105. The human brain in the head is the main command module like a main frame cumputer with the senses operating in a state of vacuum.

106. The human being is complicated but coordinated. It has 2 hearts, 2 minds, 5 senses and other components operating in the natural mode.

107. The conscious mind, the spiritual heart, and our soul, all operating in a spiritual mode.

108. All decisions are made by the conscious mind based on substance derived from the sub-conscious. The senses feed the sub with information and when validated is sent to the conscious mind to be executed.

109. Circumstances are the results of errors made, and do alter cases, do not allow other people's circumstances to disturb your life.

110. Our total existence with the exception of your soul is temporary, now is the time to decide the destiny of our being.

111. Activating and utilizing the imagination folder of the conscious mind is productive only if you exercise the will power with determination.

112. Watch your steps in the advancement of progress; it is like climbing a ladder, easier to descend than to ascend.

113. There are only 3 words in the English language that can be spelt forward or backwards and mean the same in word and meaning. "racecar" "kayak" and "level"

114. Typewriter is the longest word in the English language that can be spelt using letters on only one row of the key board.

115. The human existence is governed by laws and if any of them are violated it generates consequences.

116. The first and primary law is the laws of God. These are found in the bible and have serious consequences when violated.

117. There is a law of compensation, blessings and abundance comes through magnetic forces of gratitude.

118. There is a law of recognition, the ability of discernment is vital as true vision is sometimes disguised.

119. There is a law of prosperity, the only thing that stands between us and our portion of abundance is us.

120. There is a law of compassion, mercy has it's rewards, do not render evil for evil give a helping hand when you can.

121. There is a law of seasons, every season have a reason and every action has a reaction. Invest in doing good.

122. There is a law of placement, we inhabit a large earth. Never consider anywhere permanent, if things are not working at one location relocate.

123. There are laws of love in sequence, love God, love yourselves and love others. Love is very productive and rewarding; do not allow yourselves to be abused in the name of love

124. There is a law of success, in order to succeed we must sow seeds and the seed we sow we will reap. Prosperity is generated through generosity.

125. There are several other laws not mentioned as this is not a book of laws my mission is to point your mental consciousness in the right direction.

126. The human mind operates through visions and pictorial frames, meaning we have to create an object as a model in order to acquire it.

127. Currency is the unit through which value is transported and stored. My advice to you is make a large picture of a large bill and hang it on your wall at a conspicuous location to visualize it contineously.

128. It is of paramount importance to develop a method of magnetizing our being to absorb our blessings.

129. The destruction of society is being caused by the slow elimination of certain basic principles and values.

130. Literature is the blood of information, knowledge and is the vehicle that transports it to the human intellect to manufacure wisdom.

131. The electronic media is good but reading is more vital in the process of nourishing our human conscious minds.

132. Giving is a mean of the magnetizing process of our being. Locate an opportunity to fulfill a need, the magnitude of the vacuum measures the quantity of our reward.

133. Make time to meditate on the things of God and allow your multiple being to communicate within itself and explore new horizons to achieve rewards.

134. Unless we empower our intellect with knowledge we will loose the ability to utilize brighter horizons of success.

135. In the tranquility of the night, while our conscious mind rest in sleep, the sub-conscious mind battles with the negative forces and generate illusive dreams.

136. Marriage is an institution and for it to work we have to be committed, it is not designed to be a misunderstanding between two immature adults.

137. It was predicted that there will come a time when the old will dream dreams and the young will see visions. Prepare our intellect to receive them.

138. Invest time in our youths by having them utilizing the outdoors in fun and games, reading books and assigned chores to complete. Monitor their activities and associations, raise them in the adoration of God.

139. Make sure your words are potent in value as a bank deposit, an empty word is like a leaking container.

140. Yesterday was history tomorrow is a mystery and is promised to no one; do not allow the past to impede the progress of the future. Today is golden and is a present we should cherish it.

141. Our material possession does not determine the value of our being. Our thoughts and the good deeds that we do does.

142. The size of the gun does not determine the extent of the damage it's capable of doing, the effect of the bullet will.

143. Our life is God's gift to us, the good deeds that we do to others are our gifts to God.

144. Always give thanks to our maker and sustainer even for small mercies. Life is a obstacle course, if at any time or for any reason we fall, pick ourselves up and head to the finish line with persistence.

145. Because of all the elements involved in life's pursuit, things do not always work out the way it's planned. There are times we just have to be patient and allow them to work themselves out.

146. Never loose focus of your dreams and set your anticipations at a high altitude. Prepare your emotions to accept whatever the outcome, life goes on and there are always other opportunities.

147. There are no two absolutely identical human beings in civilization, not even if you were born twins. Everyone was uniquely made with different characteristics and capabilities to survive the duration of life.

148. Because of the compensation package there is a factor of inheritance passed down to us from deeds committed by our ancestors.

149. Everything is owned by God, the earth is the Lord's and the fullness thereof, case closed.

150. The main computer for our human existence is the brain containing our minds that produces creativity and innovations to perpetuate life.

151. The potentials of the human mind cannot be exhausted and can be utilized to benefit existence and beyon.

152. After all is said and done it is of paramount importance that we be aware of our significance and make an impact instead of wasting our lives.

153. The person we see in the mirror is just an image of us. Our true identity is in our head a section of the brain called the heart, as a man think so is he.

154. It is important to make regular assessments of our mental progress in order to make the necessary adjustments to the rotations of our minds.

155. The farming of the human conscious mind is the most lucrative means of generating material substance.

156. It is important to discern trends; literature is the life and blood of knowledge and information. The trend of disbursement is shifting from books to electronic readers. Prepare and position our intellect to absorb substance.

157. Whatever our minds conceive we can achieve by manipulating the paradigms of our mental faculties.

158. The only guarantee in life is death, live today enduring all we encounter like there is no tomorrow, as tomorrow is promised to no one.

159. When we die it is not over, there is a spiritual realm in two dimensions and the location we go is determined by the decision made by our will before we die. Seek information in the bible to make the right decisions.

160. Do unto others as you would like them do to you, always be generous in your undertakings. The good we do today will someday greet us and our ansesters as blessings in the future.

161. Always be honest in your dealings, if you receive assistance on loan, endeavor to keep the commitment and repay it.

162. Things do not always materialize as we plan it due to the possibility of interceptions by circumstances. Be conscious to accept the reality and allow it to work itself out.

163. Be careful of the people we associate with, the friends we keep impact the projection of our character.

164. Retain securely our confidential secrets, once it's disclosed there are no guarantees the distance it will travel.

165. Our mental faculty is the most valuable asset we posses, be sure to utilize it to benifit all who we encounter.

166. Always set up a foundation to carry the weight of our substance, it is not possible to carry water in a basket.

167. The formula of growth is in numeric multiplication; always devise a system to generate magnitude of units in motion.

168. The spoken word is as sharp as a sword and silences is golden, listen more and talk less.

169. Make sure the content of our utterances are factual and potent as we will be held accountable for the effects it creates.

170. Seek to establish a foundation of facts and values based on truth and potent substance. The contribution we made will serve to make an impact on the future.

171. The meeting of the minds is a constructive product through dialogue and can be utilized to benefit existence.

172. Always be alert and monitor what we consume in our bodies, it is the potency of the input that decides the products or damage to the output.

173. It is always easier to get in than to get out. Life is a one way street; do not practice making hasty decisions. Take time to ponder and weigh the pros and cons

174. Try to avoid complications, uncertainties and divisive situations. If it sounds too good to be true it's time to head for the border.

175. Be careful of the word free, although the good things in life are suppose to be free. The only thing that is free is the air that we breathe and it is polluted.

176. Our minds is fed by our senses and the processed end product will reflect its potency.

177. Think positive always and be optimistic in our anticipations think of the luxury of having a life and enjoy its privileges in paradise.

178. Let peace and love abide, do good and always be your brother's keeper. Cast our bread on the water and someday we will find it.

179. The thought to ponder is this, today is now the tomorrow we worried about yesterday. Now that it has arrived do you think it was worth the mental energy we invested?

180. Impossibility is a negative state of mind. Anything perceived is possible if all the necessary components are coordinated.

181. Consider the magnificence of nature, the earth in the form of a circular globe in orbit in the universe among several other planets. Consisting of massive bodies of water called seas, oceans, ponds and rivers, with the water cycle. To date there has never been any evidence of leakage affecting other planet in the universe, even heaven.

182. To venture is progressive, procrastination is dangerous. Always aim to progress to higher elevations.

183. Never allow the projected dark clouds of today to impede the brilliant glow of a brighter future. Give thanks to Jehovah all along the way.

184. In the still of the night and the tranquility of the moments meditate on the things of God to be like a tree planted by waters of water to bring fruits in it's season.

185. Equip yourselves with an armor of faith, truth and peace in the pursuit of life. The battle is not for the swift, but for who can endure to the end.

186. Explore our imaginations to generate innovations and perpetuate the future of existence in the remaining time.

187. Violation of rules have consequences, every action have a reaction. There is a reason for every season.

188. Envision your live through rose colored glasses, enhance it with the rays of the sunlight to acquire enormous prosperity.

189. Let our light shine in words and deeds, be not selfish in our doings, live, love and give to benefit humanity.

190. Let our light shine by erecting a mental monument with footsteps for others to follow. Never become volnorable and allow the adversary to divert you from the right pathway to the father's throne in conferance.

191. It was predicted that people will perish due to lack of knowledge, and so will it be. Seek knowledge because knowledge is power.

192. Do not allow yourself to go through life distracted by situations. Identify and enjoy the privileges to live a meaningful life to inherit paradise.

193. Today is the tomorrow we anticipated yesterday, this is the first day of the rest of our lives, cherish it. Give honor, thanks and praise to God continually.

194. It is always beneficial to seek means of improvising ways to manipulate this system of things. We can only win if we chase the evel one to flee.

195. If we sow seeds they will germinate and grow to produce fruits, likewise if we generate a thought it will eventually materialize.

196. The positive farming of the human conscious mind utilizes the potential of the intellect. Christ is Lord, oh taste and see that the Lord is good and his goodness and mercys endure forever.

197. Let us all dedicate our being to the Lord and serve him as an instrument for his purpose in peace.

198. Now that I have completed my assignment, I hope it will implement the conscious mental impact intended. Let peace and love abide.

199. We will endeavor to live and love one another and trust in God for our sustenance until the end of time comes. That's not the end there is a reserection and judgement prepared for us to eternal paradise.
200. Knowledge with experience is the beginning of wisdom, it is beneficial to seek and acquire potent knowledge from literature.

The preceding was designed to be the cake of this venture and the balance of the contents of this book to be icening on it. I will remind you that life is a gifted privilege so you must enjoy it's pleasures.

REALITIES OF LIFE

*W*e are all uniquely different in charastaristics even if we are identical twins. There are basic but essential qualities that we possess but there are people that use satan's devised equipments to deter them. Habits like indulging in using stimulants and indecent gestures that make others uncomfortable. The key element of our being is love, love God, ourselves and others like ourself. Do not be selfish in your life, consider and assist in the requirements of others as sharing is caring.

Likewise all us humans are components of the world, all connected by the air we breath thats owned by God and are placed here to occupy the earth and accomplish our unique purpose in life. At this point I wish I had the resource to publish this book in different languages as it is relevant to all humanities of this world. I will caution you that the word knowledge is viral in this publication but valuable in the realities of life.

Indulge in the acquisition of knowledge and enjoy the end products and benefits. Life is a system and a system must have components to function. Our being consist of a body with a spirit, two minds, a soul, 2 hearts, 5 sences and a conscience. The administrator of all these components are coordinated by the brain the main function equipment situated in our heads. If situations create a folder with delusions, it complicates the mind and cause it to malfunction.

All mental functions of our being are critical, do not be vulnerable when challenged with adversities in life. Utilize tolerance and listen to your mental heart. In the mathematical arena the term magnificent magnitude denotes significant amount of substance, aspire and participate in the equation. Every moment in life is a portion of our life span. Utilize them to the maximum of their potential and enjoy the benefits.

There are people that depart this life before they identify the previlages to enjoy them. It is of vital importance that we recognize and express appreciation to the creator and source of our being in prayers to him. Differentiate your wants from your needs, wants are desires and needs are necessaries. It is satisfying to acquire abundance and beneficial to share to satisfy needs. Always give thanks and praise to the source of our existence.

Habits do impact lifestyle and longevity, if we walk the pathway of prosperity we will prosper. Do not indulge in the consumption of stimulants, it will eventually manipulate your systems negatively although you feel good on the spur of the moments. The body do require nutriments, but we must be conscious of the material substances we induce in our digestive system. Insist on doing everything in moderation. Conscience influences actions, be considerate and compassionate, never allow the actions of our emotions to supersede our true personality.

Temptation to violate rules is always eminent, refrain from yielding. laws are devised for compliance. Lack of knowledge creates mental vulnerability to impede progress. Seek and acquire knowledge from potent literature, do not be vulnerable when challenged by the adversities of life. Utilize tolerance and listen to your mental heart for directives. Gold is a precious and valuable metal, while a goal is an identified mental aspiration.

When processed and achieved it determines the classification by its outcome. Our human life consist of several processes, creation, survival, redemption and extinction. Hope is a nutrisious anticipation for positive achievements. In order for a goal to be achieved in the process of life there have to be a source of sustenance. Almighty God Jehovah the father, His son Christ and Holy his Spirit that's the platform for the operating system of existence.

It is unrealistic to resent the spiritual realities of life, so I will encourage you to get your minds in motion and do not get left behind. Invest your mental impulses in positive ventures,t here is always a light beyond the tunnel. Life is wonderful if you insist on making the necessary efforts for it to be that way. I hope you will utilize the contents of this media to your benefit as intended to enrich your life on this earth. The rotations of the earth in coordination with the solar system surely impact the locations in time.

It can be detrimental if the synchronization of your mental faculties are disturbed. Time is the unit of measurement in the process of existence in the natural realm on this earth. There will be various circumstances to impede your pathway to a progressive life. I recently came in contact with someone that made me aware of some simple but critical. The word live if spelt backwards is evil, while the word lived backwards is devil thats absolutely amazing.

I will interject that it's better to get a broken heart that loosing your soul. Time is not everlasting, meaning it will be eventually exhausted. The world and the earth are two separate entities, the former in the natural will be restored by being cleansed by fire and the latter in the spiritual will last forever in paradise if we all make the righr decision. Each human was given an identity at inception but it's imperative to consciously identify your spiritual destiny by choice.

At all times try to be independent in making your own decisions, always give time for your hearts to ponder in weighing the pros and cons to avoid consequences. Be always careful in choosing your associates and be not quick to participate in their projects. I'm at the point of no return and that's my choice to be there. I've been taken this far by the hands of the Almighty to forward in this generation triomphantly. Please join me in singing a redemtion song to freedom destined for paradise.

Every human was created three dimensional consisting of a body, a soul and with a spirit. The body is natural given an allotment of time to exist to fulfill a purpose with an appointment with the eminent, death. Our souls are the most valuable asset thats indestructible based on our choices and decisions. In the persuit of life is where all the decisions are made concerning the pathway our being will travel. We must stand on Christ the solid rock as all other grounds are like sinking sand.

Although humans are not the only living creatures in time on earth, they are the most significant because we all possess a soul and mental capabilities to impact existence. Our human bodies operate in vibrations, negative and positive, while the mental system operates in rotations, forward and reverses. It is a very complicated process based on the number of different systems and their functions. Every moment in life is a portion of our life span. Try to make hay as long as you see the brilliant glow of the sun each new day.

Utilize them to the maximum of our potential and enjoy the benefits. Polarity is a component of existence, if negative interact with positive it becomes thermal, try maintaining neutrality. Always maintain consciousness to utilize your ability to discern defaults from a distance before they occur. It is beneficial to have an associate for consultance, one that you can confide in and eventually it will all fall in place. In the spiritual arena of our being, cultivate a heart with enough potency to be substantial.

The power of our human brain is immeasurable but controlled by God who is invisible. Our brains are also vulnerable to influence from the senses both negative and positive. Environmental elements can also impact conclusions. It is beninficial to allways be alert and concious to see defauits from a distant. Do not allow yourselves to be diverted from spiritual reality because of religious segregations. Get attached to christianity there is only one God.

Religions are divisive, segregative, and competitive, it's better to be focused on the ultimate authority, there's only one God. The process of life is both versatile and fragile, set the sequence of priority and always put God first in all your undertakings. The main ingredient that supports longevity to the limit is love. We must love God, love ourselves and other humans as ourselves. We were all made through a process and given an identity and option to make choices and decisions for survival.

The responsibility was put on us to recognize and utilize wisdom to make the right choices and decisions in the persuit of this life. The promises of God are sure and he said, come unto me all who are weak and heavily laden and he will compensate us with rest. Take my yoke upon you and learn of me, as my yoke is easy and my durden is light. He said study my words to be approved and you'll be compensated for your deeds.

Do not store up treasures in wrong places, be compassionate to the unfortunate ones among us to be blessed. Eventually God will say unto you, well done you good and faithful servants. You will be allowed in to acquire the strength of the Lord in joy, when I think of the goodness of Jesus and all he did for mus, my soul crys out hallilujah thank God we've been redeemed. Life without it's challenges would have a portion of emptiness, endure whatever comes along and enjoy your lives to the fullest.

It's of vital importance that we recognize and express appreciation to our maker and the source of our being. I am proud to declare with confidence that my soul is secured in Christ my Lord and King and Holy the spirit of the father that resides in me. Extend your wings to exclaim the goodness of God to us and shine a light for others to see. It's better to fly with eagles than walk with chickens to get consumed as food because of circumstances.

There is no man that have the ability to manipulate the power of God, although there are people that deceive others by performing acts in the name of God. There are televangelists that commercialize christianity, they teach false doctrin by telling people they have a false hope of going to heaven and walk the streets of glory. No human living or dead have ever been or will ever go to heaven, the only transformed one was Jesus the only begotten/adpoted son of God.

In the human body there's a nervous system, a cardiac system, a neurological system and a mental system. At this point I would like to advise you to seek and purchase a life insurance that will be beneficial for the expenses of the eminent. It is absolutely amazing seeing the beauty of nature. In time there are seasons and each season having it's advantage and some disadvantages. In the summertime most people go on vacations enjoying the beaches and other satisfying pleasures.

Depending on your location on the planet earth there are places in the winter time where there is heavy snow making it difficult to be inhabited. The human body is an individually enclosed operating system that does need maintenance occasionally. It's our responsibility to identify unusual symptoms and take the necessary actions to correct them before they become chronic. There is a time and place for everything, what's good for the goose is not good for the gander.

There are health professionals trained to intercept and make corrective measures using medications. As moments in time go by, our minds are impacted by memories, emotions, situations and anticipations. They come in both negative and positive packages and we just have to process them individually as projects. A mature mind work more efficiently and there are times when they impact our mode and sensitivity. There are nights when we will rest and dream dreams that seem real including interactions with others.

It was predicted that there would come a time when young ones will dream dreams and old ones see visions. Sooner or later we all will get there. It is of vital importance that we devote time into reaching out to people outside the realm and get them involved to expand the kingdom of God to be prepared. The factors of ethnicity and language are complicated but healthy for integration and mobility. The earth is a large planet and has enough space to accommodate all it's inhabitants.

Always be considerate of others, never be selfish in your doings. The inception of every human begin in the process of copulation, when a seed is implanted in the female womb and evolve to maturity and is born. We all were borm crying tears on our arrival and leave this life in a deep sleep.

Each human is independently assigned an allotment of time to endure a path and fulfill a purpose. Based on the age of the earth there have been several generations of humans preceding us. At present, as the average life duration is about 150 years. Knowledge have increased immensely to the point where it's my opinion that the human race have become self destructive. Please utilize your mental capabilities to acquire knowledge as it is power and power is might.

The development and experiments on chemicals on our bodies have taken us in a danger zone, and if it's not curtailed will speed our extinction. The perpetuation of life with chemicals is an industry designed to create wealth. One of my main concern is the existence of the next generation based on the direction the system of things are going and the strong influence of it's endeavors. I'm calling on all conscious minds to seek the truth from wherever it can be attained and be prepared for whatever you encounter.

If at anytime you encounter an error in this book just overlook it and move on, the bible is perceived to be the perfect word of god and I found several imperfections in it. Case in point heres one, the earth is a perfectly oval globe that revolves and it is said in the bible that it has four corners. Somewhere in this publication you'll see the results of my researches, please spend sometime to explore to verify our encounters. There are diseases that natural cures are identified but suppressed to sustain the chemical industry.

Recently my friend was diagnosed with having cancer and to satisfy his curiosity he started a research for information on the situation. During this time apparently the doctor who is involved in a network was busy making plans as to the path he would pursue in terms of treatment. The next concern was that when he had his next visit he disclosed his findings as to remedies to retard the progression of the disease. Due to the chemical warfare against the eminent which is death, the system tends not to suppress the use of natural remedies.

They at times invent alternative medications that they call generic that sometimes help and cost less usually. Most of the insurance companies paying for the medications prefer generics to curtail costs. The consumption of medications for the enhancement of life is a massive business. You will see large structural monuments erected at major intersections and at times across from each other. There are drug stores in several food stores.

I was reading an article in a natural cure magazine and discover that one of the most destructive habitual practices is indulging in stress. In most cases stress is self-inflicted by the individual based on erroneous decisions and habits. It's a good practice to not make decisions in a hurry, take time to weigh the pros and cons by your heart. Humans do have habits both negative and positive and in some cases benefit from them. A good habit is reading coupled with meditation to cultivate productive thoughts. It's beneficial to program your minds and pursue the invention of new products.

It's always good to have a friend to confide in, and keep your secrets safe. Friendship is vital to existence as it is good for someone to be there for us when needed. No one knows how much time they have to live only God knows, but in most cases extinction is advanced by destructive lifestyles and habits. There are some important facts about the human existence but taken for granted and this is it. Every human consist of a spiritual component that is indestructible and is destined for a spiritual realm when they depart this life.

There are two destinations, one is eternal life in paradise and the other is destined for total distruction with the evil one. When a child of God passes they go to be in Christ awaiting reserection to meet Christ and Jesus his representative. After there will be a judgement day, that's it for human being and it's not my intent to indoctrinate or overwhelm you but these are facts and we have to just deal with them. I am just a messenger and I am executing my assignment to your benefit.

There are opposing forces that does not want this information to get out because it reduces the results for their agenda, so at this moment I am getting a spiritual opposition. Being the controlling individual that I am, I have developed the system whereby I consult my sustainer for protection. This project was not initially designed to be what it's turning out to be, I started by trying to accumulate posts I have done on social media over a period of time.

I have been diverted by spiritual forces to accomplish this endeavor. I will persist and make sure I accomplish my assigned mission. The important thing is that we endeavor to make changes to acquire positive substance. It's very important to know that with the influences of the evil forces in opposition to the positive, there is always right and wrong, evil and good. This is not a religious book and I hope I am not overwhelming you with all this spiritual stuff, but this is all realities of life.

I do not indulge in religeons but develop a personal relationship with my maker by way of Christ my Lord. At this point I will caution you to indulge in doing the right things at all times regardless of the situations, because at some point in your existence there will be a compensation package for your deeds. Live, love and learn to tolerate your fellow men, but be observant and cautious not to be abused due to the influence of the evil forces.

It takes all kinds of people to make a world, variety is the spice of life. There are people out there who are posession of the evil adversary satan and will do what they are programmed to do to hurt us.The term human race signifies that the pathway of life would never be perfect but competitive. Strive to be a champion by devising means of legal sources of survival and be generous. Sharing is caring, indulge in it and our compensation rewards will be great.

Explore the creative sub-folders of your conscious mind and devise innovations for the enhancement of civilization.The train of life is moving right along one day at a time, make hay when the sun is shining and seek shelter when it is raining. There are several other living beings in existence on the earth but only humans have the capability and responsibility to be accountable in time for the duration of existence. At some point in the reading of my books where it will seem like I'm mentioning the same thing several times.

It's only one message but everyone's comprehention does not

work the same so I have to be creative in getting the message out. Based on the predictions in the bible, the earth will be purged and cleansed by fire for whoever choose to be an occupant of a new place called paradise that Christ and Jesus are preparing for us. There will be no more sickness or deaths but happiness in Christ the Lord. Holy/God is a mighty force to be reckoned with beyond our imagination in spirit and in truth.

The presence of God is invisible but can be felt spiritually and discerned to interact with. My purpose is not to disturb your agenda but to awake your consciousness as to the significance of your being and the assignment to accomplish your mission that is your purpose. The name of the default that we inherited and comitted is called sin and the wages of it is death, but Jesus was sent by the father God to be sacrificed as a ransom to pay the price in full by the sheding of his blood for redemption.

There is good life to live, you pick your choice but you have to make the necessary preparations. There will be lots of people that go through life and when they get to the end realized they never lived only existed. There are three things that comes not back, the spoken word, a sped arrow and a neglected opportunity. Do not allow yourselves to be distracted by divisive agendas, these are pitfalls set up by the evil one.

An umbrella works best when it's open so open your minds to achieve greatness. Seek and acquire knowledge from literature it's the beginning of wisdom not the fear of the Lord as specified in the bible. Never judge a book by it's cover because there can be a valuable treasure hidden inside. The world system is geared for the success of exploiters of the misinformed minds, retaliate with knowledge. At this point I will make an appeal to you to seek and acquire my other books and read them as the contents are designed to be mental nutrients for all conscious minds.

I can discern that in the distant future everything will be transmitted electronically and most book stores will be closed. This is a meeting of the minds and isn't it amazing? Togetherness is strength and always instills power in whatever the venture is. It is productive to practice the resentment of negatives thoughts and join me in the process of mental gratification. Promote the positives in order to achieve the progress intended, it is wise to acquire knowledge from literature and comprehend it to achieve greatness.

I will ask you again to please tolerate the word knowledge, unless you arm ourselves with knowledge you will be like a cow in the ocean without fins. At this point I will issue an advice to my Catholic friends to stop praying to the Virgin Mary asking her to pray for them at the hour of their death because she cannot. Mary was only utilized because of her purity to bring Jesus on this earth as a messenger and to be sacrificed to pay our sin debt, all the credits of his mission is attributed in Christ the Lord.

I am being tempted to go deep and elaborate on the total procedure but instead I will encourage you to research the bible as it illustrated in it's entirety. No one goes to the father Jehovah God but through Christ, he is the only way and not in Jesus's name. Life was given to us to accomplish a mission for a purpose within a given amount of time. My main assignment is to share the words of God among the lost heathens in order to bring them to reality to expand the kingdom of God when it comes.

They are required to submit their being to Jesus and be baptized by submersion in water in the name of the father Jehovah, the son Christ and Holy his spirit. The main ingredient in the endeavor is substance, seek and devise means of acquiring it. Again I am appealing to you to dream big dreams and work toward achieving them. You must develop the capabilities of discernment to identify them and wait with great anticipations.

The height of greatness will not be attained by sudden flight but while others are asleep they toiled and meditate on the things of God. The gift of Almighty God Jehovah is eternal life. I will encourage you to pursue the pathway to achieve the gold as the sky is the limit. Time is a precious commodity but is temporary, there is good life to live and enjoy in the pursuit if you choose to follow the right pathway trusting in Jehovah God by way of Christ.

To quilify for the previlage of acquiring everlasting life in paradise you must get saved by grace through faith and be redeemed by Jesus's blood. It's a requirement to accept and submit yourself to him by grace and get submerged in his cleansing blood to be forgiven of your sins. Once that's accomplished you are a child of God and a sheep of his pasture. Getting saved is a gift from God with a ribbon filled with mercy and blessings in it.

Whenever we pray to God do it by the only way through Christ and not in Jesus's name.

Jesus is our messiah, redeemer, saviour, comforter and king of the jews, the seed that made him was extracted by Holy the spirit from Christ who implanted it inside the virgin Mary to born the son of man. Thereby Jesus is a decendant and representative of christ but not a member of the trinity. Religions teaches otherwise as their leaders are agents of satan. Oh taste and see that the Lord is good in three dimentions, his goodness and mercies will endure forever.

Christ our Lord, life and salvation is identified as the Spirit and Truth, he's the only way to approach the throne of grace with our prayers and suplications to the father. There are evidence that God operates in polarity based of his tolerance of the evil adversary, to prove his authority. God will not allow heaven and earth to pass away so the message must go out to the world with his words.

This must be accomplished to bring in souls to expand his new kingdom on the new earth. Redemption draws near so the world will get rescued to be saved by Jesus's blood. There is an invitation to all those who are sick and heavily laden to submit their beings and get rest in God in three dimension. Nature including vegitation is magnificiant and is controlled by God it's creator but man intervein emencely. It flurishes under water and thats why it survived the flood with Noah.

This earth is destined to be distroyed by fire because of sin, it's evident that vegitation will be extinguished. That signifies that the new earth will be barren. The limb on an human body named the head is the most versetile, complicated and essential control center of our existence. It consist of all five senses, one heart, two minds, and our spiritual being with our soul. Our head is similar to a vacuum as it absorb one hundred percent of the substantial requirements for our survival.

Today is uniquely special as it's the first day in the rest of our lives, let us give thanks and praise to Almighty God the sustainer of our lives. Jesus is not God he is a representative of God, there's no place in the bible that you will see that God spoke as he is invisible and does not utter. Jesus was utllized to vocalize God which includes his inspirations by his spirit to the writers of the bible and other authors including myself.

When Jesus uttered that "I am the way truth and life, no one goes to the father but by me" that was Christ speaking through him. There's nothing God cant do and it was predicted that Christ the Word would becone flesh to dwell on the earth for a season. The vergin Mary an human was implanted with a seed from Christ by Holy the Spirit of God, when that pregnancy matured Jesus was born as a son of man. He was given an assignment by the father to accomplish, and he did it.

The father was well pleased because of his accomplishments and beggotten/adopted him as a son.

MISSION ACCOMPLISHED

Based on my research I have concluded that mortal life is a process and like any other process it require substantial amount of resource in order to produce products and along the way dispose of waste. Please come along with me in the exploration of the spiritual aspects of our being. We all were made by a powerful maker and sustainer in a process and indevidually have a predestined process to pursue our timed adventure. Almighty God the ruler of the universe exist eternally in three dimentions and is in total control in the the process called exestence.

Here we go, In the beginning God was a sole entity existing in the secret place of the most high in realms of glory charged with the power of his spirit who's name is Holy. He then created the universe with all the planets including heaven, the earth and several others, he then put the earth in rotation and began the clock of time. Almighty God chose the planet earth to establish the process of human existence. God then created the angelic beings on planet heaven and chose one named Michael to be his representative.

Another of the angels violated his authority by defecting and became in oposition to God and was given the name Lucifer. Ever since that incident there have been a confrontation of the forces, evil and good.The next thing he did was to Create the first male human and named him Adam, it was obvious to the father that Adan needed a companion so he created a mate for him but the female was somewhat more brilliant than Adam, so God pulled back because that was not the way he planned it.

I will remind you that I'm just a researcher sharing my findings with you, I forgot her name and never heard of her again. Ok here we go, God chose the planet earth to be inhabbited by humans. He made Eve from the dust of the earth and implanted a portion of Adam's mentallity in her, here is where we identify her imperfection. God had put the next stage which is putting copulation on hold. Lucifer, remember him? he convinced Eve to disobey the rules of God so he could implant a seed in her, he did and she ended up having twins a boy and girl.

The boy's name was Cain and the girl's was Lulluwa, existence continued to the point where the restrictions were realeased and Adam copulated with Eve and she eventually had another set of twins. the names of the new twins were Able and Acklea, and she was more attractive than the first sister. When all the children became matured and was ready for mating, the parents crossed them so able got the more attractive sister. That caused Cain to become jealous, they went out in the fields one day and Cain killed his brother able.

It was predicted that the Word who is Christ and the second of the trinity of God would become flesh and dwell among us on earth as a human. Eventually when the earth became inhabited God identified a virgin name Mary from a reputable family and decided to have the Holy spirit implant a seed in her. If you are observant you will see it's the second time a seed was implanted inside a female by a spirit. When the baby was born from Mary, he was given the name Jesus as he was sent here to do the will of father.

Jesus was sent here by the father to pay the sin debt we inherited all the way back from Eve and Cain plus those we committed. In my research. During the period when Jesus was human on earth he had a soul like all humans and a spirit, he was empowered and protected by Holy the spirit of God and accompanied by Christ. This is my opinion, the bible is a unique history book containing some words of God and most of what transpired throuhout the ages including the life of Jesus.

There were several writers involved in the establishment of the bible and several of them disclosed their personal opinions on situations and issues. My opinions are inspirations from higher powers. I have dedicated my being as a sponge to absorb, document and share the substance with humanity to expand God's kingdom on this earth.The father utilized Jesus his begotten/adopted son to do mericles and eventually pay the ultimate price for us humans.

I can imagine how defeated he felt in the process of the crucifiction, but it had to be done it was the will of God. Christ in the combination is the second portion of the trinity in the equation. I will reinterate again that in order to aproach the throne of grace to communicate with the father in spirit and truth. Neither Jesus or Mary his mother were spirits, they had souls. Jesus was transformed to be a spirit in order to be admitted in heaven.

Christ is the ultimate of that process and all that Jesus accomplished were through Christ, he is Lord. I will encourage those of us who have'nt submitted their being to Christ through Jesus to be born again, because we must do that to enter the kingdom. As I approach the completion of my assigned venture there are some basic principles I must instill in you. The main one is the development of your capabilities of discernment to visualize and set goals to achieve. In the pursuit of life there are parameters of curtailment and timing to abide by. There are moods and modes, they sound similar but different.

Moods are products of our emotions, while modes are set standards. we are an independent entity and should be treated as such only emulate people that impress you positively. Create our own modes and stay within the boundaries of your resources. Seek and enjoy means of fun and enjoyment to cause joy and laughter as they are food for your souls. In the misty moonlight, beneath the glowing star lights everything will be allright as long as we are in control. The human body does go through different phases and there are different processes to restore normalcy, like rejuvenation and restoration.

It's of vital importance that we sleep for our minds to recouperate, we do have a very creative mentality and is always seeking situations and circumstances to explore. I only speak the english language and ran into a guy that made me aware of much and I will share it with you. Here are some technicalities it is improper to say in the english language "I is" or "I are" but yours truly is skillful to manipulate the formula. "I is" the number nine letter in the alphabet and I know a guy that his initials are "IR" you see codes can be broken. Here are some thoughts to ponder.

- There are no eggs in eggplant or ham in hamburger neither is there pine in pineapple.
- English muffins were not invented in England nor French fries in France.
- Boxing rings are square not round and guinea pigs are not from Guinea nor are they pigs.
- A slim chance and a fat chance are similar but a wise man and wise guy are opposites.
- Your house can burn up while it burns down and you will fill in a form by filling it out.

- * There is no dog meat in hot dogs.
- * Computers were developed by the human race in a stationary mode.
- * Sweet breads which are not sweet but mints and sweet meats are candies.

Check this out, These are words that are spelt the same but have different meanings. A "bass" that is a fish was painted on a "bass" drum that is an instrument.

There is no time like the "present" so it's time to send the "present" it's a gift.

The man shot at the "dove" a bird and to avoid being killed it "dove" in the bushes.

The garbage dump was so full they had to "refuse" the full amount of "refuse".

And this is it.......

Why is it that writers write and fingers do not fing, grocers do not groce and hammers do not ham. If a vegetarian eat vegetables a humanitarian should eat humans.

I will encourage you again to acquire means that promotes laughter as it is food for the soul. It is perfectly normal to apologize when we are wrong and say sorry. Stay clear of eminent danger and do not provoke the possibility of premature extinction. Life is a timed venture.

The foundation of life is erected on pillars of principles that I will be illustrating in this section. Guard our attitude with our lives because we will never get a second chance to make a first impression. Do not allow yourselves to indulge in falsehood either in words or deeds, our words should be as credible as a bank deposit.

Do not promote any gesture unless you can authenticate it's source. Practice the art of meditation using your mind to cultivate mental gems. Always aspire attaining higher elevations, do not stay in the realm of neutrality. This equation will cause you to think numeric, 2+2=4 and 2X2=4 you are going no where. In the arena of nature we can use the color of the clouds to determine the possibility of moisture, behind every dark cloud there is a silver lining.

The train of life is moving right along one day at a time, make hay while the sun is shining and seek shelter when it's raining. Carefully utilize the pathway of life utilizing the allotment of time to our ultimate destination based on the decisions we made. This book was designed to be a manual for living a meaningful life. In this life it is beneficial to resent negative confrontations.

At this late stage of my existence I will confess to you that I am electronically sustained in existence. I have lived a life consisting of substantial achievements, and is convinced that all us humans were made and assigned here to accomplish a mission like having a blueprint as to the pursuit of life's journey. It is of vital importance that we invest in the magnitude of our true profile of appearance in order to acquire respect.

We should erect a monument that others seek to emulate with

our spiritual heart, use adequate proportion of Peace, love, unity, compassion, generosity and respect. Get involved in ventures to magnetize your being to acquire financial substance, it is the foundation for material success. Let us all acquire the spiritual status to qualify for life everlasting in paradise.

The world occupies the earth in different locations in different colors creed and languages. The world system is devised by the evil one to distract us in order to travel a pathway to destruction to sustain his agenda. A new day is dawning where knowledge will increased for us humans to discern the traps so we can evade them.

Learn to be conservative by developing systems to multiply and retain the nest eggs of the ventures. Currency is the liquid stream for material substance and serves as a vehicle for resource, be a magnet for resource. The next two and most important principles are choices and decisions. Be very careful of the choices you make as all that glitter is not gold and never make decisions in a hurry. Always weigh the pros and cons by giving your hearts and minds an time to make the right determinations.

Time and time again people jump the gun and end up suffering the consequences instead of reaping the benefits. Our presentation is vital and our impression is critical as they display our true identity. Be careful not to get rich because it's easier for a camel to make it through a needle's eye than a rich man to obtain a ticket to paradise.

The maintenance of our dental faculties is essential as your smile discloses the mode of your invisible spiritual heart. The most important element of our smile is a brilliantly white set of teeth. Everyone is unique in their own way in all aspects in terms of preferences and likenesses. One person likeness is another one's dislikes and that is why variety is the spice of life and required. I am a very creative person and like to experiment in order to acertain my curiocities.

I can remember there was a time I experimented on foods by having a different country food every night and it was much fun. I have since experimented and is able to prepare several different foods by myself. The most versatile meat is chicken and secondly is pork, but the key to the taste and satisfaction is in the seasoning. This publication will be a treat for your vocabulary and will be like a personal manual for us on our life's journey. Relationships originate from admiration and desires and can be very delicate in nature.

Marriage is an institution and in order for it to be successful both partners must be committed. Children are our future and should be products from a family marital environment. We should nurture and raise children in the admeration of God and by instilling positive value and principles in them so when the mature they will be secured. Children must be monitored as to the company they keep and their educational grades and progress. Devote time to assist them in doing homework assignments and projects.

Reward yourselves by devising situations, moments of leisure and entertainment to cause fun, joy and laughter as these are food for your soul. Do not be selfish in your doings be on the look out to satisfy deserving needs. Avoid complaining because it does not matter what the situation might be there is someone having it worse. Always make time to give thanks to our creator and the sustainer of our being. Due to the differences in opinions there will always be disagreements.

It's not benificial to get involver in any debates, never go to the point of confrontation respect the opinions of others even if you disagree. Because of our vulnerability we are subjected to the influences of the evil forces. Never cultivate envy in your mental heart to the point of devising a process of revenge or retaliation. Keep your nose out of other people's situations and concerns.

Do not get involved in other people's business as you have enough of our own to work with. Keep a smile on our face projecting an illumination of peace, love and unity. Avoid repeating what someone else said as there will be times when it has negative consequences and get attached to you unfortunately. The sun will come up tomorrow but there is no guarantee you will see it as tomorrow is promised to no one.

Communication is a very important element in our existence and whoever invented the cellulor phone should be given an award for excellence. I can remember the time when our only means of distant contact was through ma--bell with lines on poles by the wayside. As kids we used to connect cans with cords and play phones. I often wonder how did we exist without the cell-phones, then we got the beepers.

Now that technology is advanced to the point where we can communicate by sending texts including pictures. The key to success is acquiring knowledge from literature with substance and utilizing it efficiently. The power of the human mind is elaborate and cannot be measured based on our source and sustenance. Over time in life some people develop habits and that's fine as long as they maintain them within limits and in moderation. My neighbor is a lover of pets and devotes his leisure time to his pet dogs.

Recently I discovered that he sleeps in the bed with five dogs, holy smoke that is no joke, give me a break that is outside the limits. It takes all kinds of people to make a world and different strokes for different folks. A destructive habit is the induction of mental stimulants in the body. Coffee, alcohol and tobacco are not good and over time cause problems and sometimes fatality. In the pursuit of life we will acquire an accumulation of substance of value in both liquid and solid forms.

This is beneficial as they can be disposed of to get compensation to assist in the golden stage of life. It's also important to acquire life insurance earlier in life to take care of the expenses of the eminent. I will advise you to periodically take an inventory of your deeds on your life's journey and seek to acquire knowledge to energize them. There are times when the issues of life seem strange but we must realize we are involved in an experiment.

I will erinterate that if you should see anything mentioned here more than once, overlook it as repetition cause attachment to the mind. Anticipation is a product of seeds you sow, invest in positive ones in order to acquire enormous rewards. If you do not have a vision of an aspired future, you are like a tree without roots and will not bare fruits. Life is a process and in order to be successful you must acquire knowledge and participate. The race is not for the swift but for who can endure to the finish line, persistence is the name of the game.

The root word for knowledge is the word know, if you do not know technically you are impeared. The pathway of life is like you going on a road trip in your car to a strange location without a GPS or road mop with the directions. If at anytime you should come to an intersection you will confusingly wonder which way to go. Self-empowerment with knowledge are vital commodity in the formula for success. It is important to monitor the contents of what we consume in our bodies.

In order to keep up with the population explosion there are certain destructive chemicals used as preservatives. The processes of attraction are alive and well, seek and acquire knowledge at an early age to reap the benefits later. Insist on feeding your conscious minds with mental nutrients while it's emotions fluctuate in the autumn breeze. Last time I checked I realize that people with money did not work for it, instead they had the money work for them, or inherited it. Devise and market goods or services, gamble and win or steal it.

Honesty is the best policy like a tree it bears fruits, the spiritual heart and mind operates either open or closed, it is beneficial to have them function in the former. An open mind seeks to grasp opportunities and utilize it's capabilities to establish them, while an open heart consists of compassion. The formula of multiplication is the source of enormous substantial magnitude. Premeditation is healthy for the mind, it's somewhat like fertilizer to generate and promote progress. Our brain is the most powerful instrument in the process of our being.

Never allow your being to become stagnant, seek and acquire means of expantion in numeric magnitude. Although there is a resource factor in the equation, there is good life to live. The vision of numeric magnitude is very attractive and rewarding, go whatever distance is required to acquire it. In the age that we are living in, a healthy life is a treasure due to the processing of our intake with chemicals as preservative.

Currency is the backbone of material sustenance, it is the chief resource and the foundation for support. Life is a challenging process for a duration of time and based on the worldwide divisive systems we must rely on our sustainer for guidance. One of the most beneficial means of governing is democracy, whereby the majority of people make the decision as to the leadership. Based on the scale and rate of the development of technology everything is computerized.

People have learned the art of manipulating computers whereby causing a default. Recently in the USA 2019 the incident explained in the previous paragraph occurred and the system is destined to go in a negative and destructive direction. Love is lovely and war is ugly, the new administration is resurrecting the nuclear arms agenda. There are other world powers jumping on the bandwagon as defense, which is dangerous. I am a positive individual and try at all times to pursue a pathway to progressive, rather than head toward destruction.

I believe we should stand firm and honor our commitments in life, there are medals of reliability to be achieved. Because of the lack of wisdom, the percentage of the unfortunate and destitute people is higher than the progressive. This book was written as a manual to point and guide the masses in the right direction to enjoy life to the fullest. This concept of progression is based on the masses making the right decisions early in life as to the direction to go to living a productive and progressive life.

At this stage of existence it is more productive to concentrate on the predictions in the bible as to how to comply. The words of God is light to our path in getting to know him and show others, to build his kingdom that his will be done. I will remind you that there will be a reward of everlasting life as long as we make the right choice of accepting Jesus as our savior, and invite Holy the spirit to take up residence in our spiritual hearts.

I will advise you to introduce this book to all your family, friends and associates for them to acquire a copy for their information and spiritual benefits. It is of vital importance to reserve time to meditate and cause your mental faculties to communicate with each other for coordination in making right decisions. What better way to spend our entire future than acquiring life on the new earth name paradise forever?

I have personally experienced the importance of being persistent in the pursuit of life, the proper procedure in being successful to aspere the goal and be patient. Again the word Lord is a title, like a king, queen or other monarchy, there are false gods. In my island home Jamaica there is a cult that recognized Haile Selassie from Africa as Jah meaning God and worship him as such. My God has a name and His name is Jehovah, may we praise, honor and worship his holy name.

There is a personal subject I would like to elaborate on before departure and this is it. Freedom is a vital part of our existence and especially in the USA we are allowed to utilize it within limits, due to the rapid expansion of technology there are the possibilities of interventions.The three main elements are desires, choices and decisions, there are others. The two main restrictions that prevent accomplishments are laws and lack of resources. The super spiritual hi-way have no preventions is the way to an everlasting life on the new and purified earth called paradise.

Comprehension is the key to the brain for us to comply with the requirements. I was given this assignment and I have done an immense amount of efforts to accomplish the mission by giving all who are exposed to this information an option to choose. To prove to you the importance of this project, I have had sleepless nights when information comes in my brain and I have to respond by getting up to document them.

There are times when I reread the contents of my books in amazement as to where these information came from. Let us all give thanks to God Almighty Jehovah for using me as a vessel to convey this information to you that his will be done. At all times be sure that you are on the lookout with discernment to identify opportunities. It is a onetime chance as they will not return. A critical aspect of our being is our feelings which are based primarily on the contentment of our minds.

There are several kinds of feelings some are rewards of satisfaction from desires and situations. Do not react negatively to a feeling based on false assumptions. Acquire and utilize potent mental substance to keep the brain stabilized. Deception is damaging but can be discerned and resented. Supersede the normal status by exploring the platform to perfection and exceed expectations. The numeric agenda can be easily manipulated due to the rapid development of technology, whereby people with financial substance can be successful.

My insinuations make an impression on your minds enough to put it in motion, and your aspirations will be achieved. At this stage in time we need to dream big dreams and aim for reaching higher elevations in existence. We must hope that prosperity will fall like rain and our efforts will grow like trees that blossom and bear fruit. My appeal to conscious humans is to pick themselves up and not be a victims, put your trust in the Almighty God Jehovah because he is able to sustain us for his purpose to expand his kingdom.The two most important component of the human being are the spiritual heart, soul and mind.

The mind is a creative processor of information and the spiritual heart is an effective communicator. Both are located in the brain, do not render evil for evil because compassion is of more value than retaliation. The forces of evil thrive on our negligence by ignoring basic principles of a meaningful life. There are people that indulge in evil practices like listening to fortune tellers for future predictions. Protect ourselves from sunlight and meditate in the moonlight. Lay up spiritual treasures by sowing seeds to fulfil needs.

There are people with problems controlling their ego and will try to invade your space. Do not allow yourselves to be manipulated by anyone, always maintain a high esteem. It's good in certain situations to seek advice, although not all bring the right result as circumstances alter cases. Try to be generous in your endeavors, there will be a compensation for your kind deeds. I have recently done a review of the products of my mind here and is convinced that God is utilizing the instruments of my intellect like he did to Solomon, the only difference is I am unable to sing the songs of Solomon.

Life is surely a wonderful privilege and we should all give thanks to God our sustainer by way of Christ the only true pathway to access and communicate with Jah. God is invisible, no one have seen him at anytime but he can be discerned spiritually. All humans have an appointment with death but the time is unknown, and we all have sinned and come short of our original requirements but Jesus paid the price.

Jehovah God sent his only begotten son to be sacrificed to pay for our sin debt in full, all we have to do is request through prayer in spirit and truth by way of Christ. Unfortunately the god of this world satan have had his people removed the name of Jehoveh from the king james version of the bible and replaced it with the title Lord, that's fine. Patients is a virtue and persistence will conquer resistance to initiatives developed from aspired ventures. All major achievements originated from a thought, a product of the conscious mind that is pursued to be accomplished.

It is of vital importance to determine and project our true identity, sometimes the individual we assume we are is not real. Our true identity can be projected as being mightier than is imagined, the reality remains ambiguous until discovered. Every human does have a system of limitations, whenever that limit is reached there is an alarm meaning it's time to seek maintenance by treatment. I will encourage you to share this experience exploring the contents of this media with family, friends and associates so they can acquire their own copy to enjoy by visioning the realities of life.

The instruction we were given was to seek the kingdom of

God and all it's righteousness and all things will be added. At this stage of this venture it's my duty to acknowledge the recognition of your presence and congratulate you on the accomplishment of your assignment. I am confident that your minds will be reformed based on the absorption of the potency of the contents. Time is of the essence and as time go by it's essential to practice and benefit from the substance derived here. There are numerous aspects of the information in the contents that will positively reform your lives and divert it to security. If you should have an assessment done of your mental capabilities you will realize that there are still room for expansion.

Silence is golden but the spoken word is mightier than a sword, when uttered cannot be retracted. The following are mental nutrients to feed the mind and fertilize it's productivity enduring the realities of life pursuit. Life is a one time expedition with gifted privileges for us to utilize to our benefit. I am convinced that a mighty force is utilizing my mind to impact vulnerable minds worldwide seeking knowledge, and impacting them with substance. The human brain is the command center.

MENTAL NUTRIENTS

*T*here are several history books with records of the past there are several different translations of the bible, it contains words from God. Instructions, commandments, predictions and accomplishments are all documented for our reference. I will encourage everyone to acquire and read my books for aditional directives. In the process of acquiring knowledge you must utilize discernment of facts. Be aware that there are two forces continually competing for the control of our being and trying to eventually acquire our souls.

Satisfaction is an accomplishment of anticipation and comes straight from the heart, there will be times when you will be disappointed based on the outcome. Nature possesses enormous amount of capabilities that are not being utilized. The sun emits light by day, likewise the moon glows light by night. It's benificial to make meditation a routine, day and night. It was promised that we will be like a tree planted by the rivers of water to bear fruit.

Our total being, heart, mind, soul and spirit are in our brain in our head. The brain is supplied with information by the sences and sustained by love with respect. It is very productive to utilize your mind in secluded quiet time to generate innovative ideas to be compensated. Two of the most crucial elements in the pursuit of life are choices and decisions. It is of vital importance that we do a mental assessment of our deeds so as not to encounter possible negative consequences.

Each and every human without disabilities are blessed with a degree of flexibility for survival. Utilize your tallents to identify, attain, accumulate and retain substance for your benefit. Do not allow because of lack of knowledge your mental intellect to be intercepted by diversive indoctrination from the evii one. I will reinterate that respect and love are two important elements of life, and sharing is caring. Please share the substance and experience of this venture with your friends and associates.

Experimentation is an important aspect of life based on your capability to identify and achieve correct results, experience teaches wisdom. Outside the rapid expansion of technology, it would seem everything otherwise is experiencing deterioration or having a logging trend. These are signs of the time. There are times when you will get hurt, more severly by love ones. Do not improvise ways to retaliate, instead generate and sing a song of love in your heart.

I will bring you to the realization of the importance of your demeanor, please realize that our face impression is capable of displaying our state of mind. Our mental heart goes through numerous phases based on the circumstances we encounter. Never get involved in any stressful situations, keep in close relationship with Jehovah through Christ and he will work things out. Do not carry any malice, envy, grudge or intent of retaliation for anyone.

Maintain a clean heart and spirit and cast all our cares on God because he cares for us. Recently I have been surprised at somethings I found mentioned in the bible, these are things going on in the world today. It is important and beneficial that we talk to all our friends and associates making them aware that this is not it. There is an option to seek and achieve the hope of everlasting life on the new earth promised by God called paradise to who make the right choice.

The security of your spiritual being is essential, seek to acquire the hope of being in paradise. Try to identify a need and try to supply the requirements to satisfy it and be blessed. It is always better to give than receive, it is my desire to reach out to the unsaved to expand Jehovah's kingdom, comfort is nutrient for our mental faculties so it can function more effectively. Otherwise it is like trying to take a swim where there is no water.

Life is a process with challenges, there are no two similar human even if you were born twins. There is never two similar days, weather it rains or shine. There is no perfection in civilization. Make the best of life today. I do appreciate the participation of everyone here and encourage you to have all our friends and associates acquire a copy of this book. I am inspired by the ultimate authority to accomplish this mission. We all were sent here to accomplish a mission, no one knows what there's is.

The gurantee is that sometime in the pursuit of your life you will do something significant to substantiate it. We welcome the dawning of every new day and should always tell someone that you love them. Love and respect are the two main elements of our being. My advice to you is once you descern an opportunity in life do not procrastinate, acquire it. Opportunities usually knock on the door of life once, in the process of life it's beneficial to germinate goals and work to achieve them. Submit yourselves to be guided by the sustainer of life.

Our soul are the most valuable and potent element of our being, let's empower it with confidence and security in God. In the still of the night and the tranquility of the moments, meditate on the words of God and be like a tree planted by the rivers of water. We will bear fruit in it's season and whatever we do will prosper. We have gotten to the point in time where civilization is deceived by the evil forces and deterred by the mention of the source of our existence.

Warning, get out of babylon and seek refuge in Almighty God by way of Christ to acquire the hope of eternal life in paradise. The largest planet is the earth and it rotates in orbits for humanity known as the world to acquire the benifits from the sun and moon. There's only one heaven and it's occupied by the angelic and spiritul forces of God. Every moment of time in the pursuit of life is precious and should be treasured. The suprising factor is that there is another life promised by our maker, but requires a procedure based on our decisions.

Please do not allow the evil forces to invade your minds and deter you from the substance you derive from the inspirations being distributed by the appointed people of God.The bible stipulates that the fear of God is the beginning of wisdom, fear here means respect and love, go for it! The word Lord is a title, like king, queen, president etc. Lucifer is the god of this world system of things and it's being dangerously deceiving the world with false indoctrinations in religions.

There's only one true and living God in three dimensions, Almighty God's name is Jehovah, he is omnipotent and omnipresent. He is the creator of the universe and it's contents. Jehovah is the father and executive and sustainer of life. He can be accessed through his son Christ and Holy his powerful Spirit. Now that we have formally achived disclosure of God's true identity, I will encourage you to pursue the means of being attached and secured in him. The words of God in the bible will be a light to your pathway to him.

The power of the human mind is immeasurable, everything in existence other than the elements of nature was derived from a mental thought. Everything that's implicated can be substanciated based on predictions.The process of life is both versatile and fragile, set a sequence of priorities, always putting God first. Do not allow yourselves to be diverted from spiritual reality because of religious segregation We have total access to God through Christ.

Jonah was sent to Ninivy to warn that nation and here I am subtituting him. I am convinced that I've been appointed to share the words of God in the process of reaching the uttermost parts of this earth, to expand God's kingdom that his will be done and the end of time will come. When I think of the goodness of Jesus and all he have done for me my soul cries out halleujah, thank God I am one of the chosen. Blessed be the tides that bind our hearts in christian love.

Amazing grace how sweet the sound that saved a wretch like me I once was lost but now I'm found, was blind but now I am able to discern my destiny through Jesus who paid the ultimate price for my imperfections. The acknowledgement of Christ the Lord is the beginning of wisdom which is derived through discernment of potent literature. Come let us all meditate and try to accomplish the will of the Lord. Our mental capabilities of reasoning in conjunction with discernment of God's instructions, will illuminate our pathway to acquiring our hope of paradise.

I will compliment you for your patience and tolerance in acquiring the impact of this substance for the duration of our existence. My greatest wish is for God to curtail the ability of the evil adversary to having access to our minds. Joy is a precious commodity that is acquired through our mental perseptions to enhance our hope in living a meaningful life. God is the owner of our breath and the ruler of our destiny and we must continually give him thanke and praise.

Anticipations are productive as salvation is our hope of paradise to keep our dreams alive. Never give up on them, hold on for life. Every day of life is valuable, it's of paramount importance that we design a fruitful plan to accomplish our hope to inherit paradise. In my ventures I hope to initiate a thought that will culminate into something of significance to benifit future generations and be blessed. I have submitted my being to my maker to be used for his purpose to expand the kingdom that his will be done.

Sleeping is a journey and no one know their destiny, it is suprising when one gets to a new day. Give thanks always to our sustainer of life. Efficiency is useless if allowed to be dormant, utilize all potent capabilities to be classified as being productive. Our words, actions and demeanor projects our true being and character. Everyone was given the capability to conserve and accumulate resources for survival. Always be compassionate and help to satisfy genuine needs. Be sure that our conservative agenda does not curtail your generosity and compassion.

Utilize your mental resources productively, everything in existence originated from a seed of thought. The most versatile state of our being is liquid so we need to consume adequate amount of water daily. Hopes, dreams, wishes and promises contain a degree of uncertainty. Be positive and anticipate the best from our main source Almighty God. Gestures consisting of the words love, happiness and unity promotes an environment of togetherness and pleasure.

Seek knowledge from potent literature and acquire wisdom to impact existence and beyond. It is of vital importance that we keep our minds active to sustain it's capabilities to produce substance from our thoughts. i will shaire my experience with you, there are times when I have sleepless nights in order to document material that enter my mind. The human brain has the capability to curtail functions of the body based on the quality of substance derived from the senses.

Of course there is no one perfect so there are times when we make wrong decisions and suffer the consequences. It's important that we reserve moments in time to relax and listen to music because the sound of music relaxes the mind. Always be careful not to become vulnerable because the evil one can invade our mental faculties. If you reach this far in this book, you are on the right pathway. Allow today to go down in history as the past, for it to be read about by the next generation. Let us anticipate the mystery of a brighter tomorrow, although tomorrow is promised to no one because we all are predestined.

A human life is the culmination of a process with decisions and choices to be made before they die, because it was appointed to all human to die. My main purpose of this venture is to replenish the mind so the heart can function effectively to assist in our decisions and choices. The acquisition of satisfaction is an accomplishment of anticipations developed by our hearts. A desire is a necescity generated by our hearts, to acquire it we got to go get it. It is a one way street to the city of happines and satisfaction.

The spiritual heart is a vital component of the being, it plays the most important part in decision making. Be consistent with time as it is spontaneous and of vital importance to synchronizing actions in moments. Satisfaction is a reward for improvised acts within boundaries of reason to cause pleasure. The process of life does have limits to abide by to prevent mishaps. Greatness is a state of mind based on achievements and should not be abused. Moderation is adequate for normalcy and destiny is a reality of life, we can not rule our destiny.

Our being is monitored and sustained from inception to extinction by Almighty God. The congestion of ones brain is detrimental because it's the main computer that moniters and controls our existence. I will again imply that efficiency is useless if allowed to be dormant. Everyone was given the capability to conserve and accumulate substance. Always be compassionate and help to satisfy genuine needs. Be sure that your conservative agenda do not curtail generosity and compassion. Always contribute to be blessed. Utilize all your potent capabilities to be classified as being productive.

In this endeavor I hope to initiate a thought that will culminate into something of significance to benefit minds in the future and be blessed. The total numeric depletion of worldly existence is inevitable, so it is of vital importance to acquire the necessary spiritual credentials in preparation for the new realm. This world is under the control of satan, if you are living a life without problems you are on the wrong pathway. My advice to you is to make a quick u-turn. Whenever tears fall down like rain be sure it have the correct category tag, there are tears of sadness and tears of joy.

I will compliment you for your tolerance of my mind's production, every opportunity I get I use it to cultivate my mind for your benefit. My advice to you is to make the best of your life, as you know not when it will end. It was appointed to all humans once to die, and after death there will be a judgement for your wrong deeds. My advice to you is to choose the corret final destination. The longevity of human's life is being done by doctors practicing, using technology with chemicals and is being successful.

Human life is determined by sounds or actions, extinction is caused by consuming poisonous or toxic substances. It's of vital importance to develop and mentain nesteggs, as in the pursuit of life there will be rainy days. Success is attained through efforts with persistence, always set goals and work to achieve a positive outcome.

How good and pleasant it is for us all to dwell in piece, love and unity, it's like moving a mountain by faith.

Segregation is a devisive instrument, we are all one connect by air regardless of religion, nationality or skin color. Joy happiness and piece of mind are vital elements of life, be sure when you cry they are tears of joy. There are laws of God, laws of man and laws of nature, always be subjective so as not to suffer the consequences of violations. The virbal utterances of our mouths are versetile commodities, they can cause pleasure, laughter, pain and food for our brain. Always make a intensive assesment of them before you utter because once they are disbursed they cannot be retracted.

God rules and administrate our destiny from inception to extingtion, it cannot be planned, hope for or selfdetermined.

ESSENTIAL INTERJECTIONS

I will imply that it's benificial to get to know the components of our being. Every human consist of two hearts, two minds, five sences, one body, one spirit and one soul. There are several organs all working together to sustain the complecated process called life, it's important to moniter what we consume into our digestive system. A state of the mind is more critical than a state of the heart. One mind is conscious while the other is subconscious, but there can be a meeting of the minds.

A state of mind can place an impact on our normal body functions in terms of responces. A state of the mental heart in the brain adjacent to the minds, exibits skills, creativity and can generate credits, rewards and mental satisfaction. The physical heart is basecally a pump that circulates blood throughtout our bodies with oxygen and neutrients. God is our maker and sustainer, he owns our breath and rules our destiny.

I'm convinced that procrastination is a virus that's detrimental to progress, due to the symptoms identified in the development process. There are implications disclosed by experts to utilize alternatives that will expedite a successful outcome. There are intersections on the information super hi-way that's strategically placed to impede the velocity of the anticipated growth. My mind do possess the capability to cultivate perceptions in the process of dominating all oppositions.

It was previously predicted that there will come a time when there will be critical acts of nature and devastation in divers places. Scientists have assumed that it's being activated by interferance with the earth's infrastructure. There are in the process of explorations based on the demand for energetic resources. The time have arrived in this year 2020 it's imperative that we God's people seek refuge in the hands of the Almighty. These are signs of the time.

When peace like a river assend our way and sorrows like sweet billows roll. Whatever our lot oh God, you have thought us to know it is well with our soul. Our peace is our state of mind maintained by meditation on the things of God and rellying on his promises. The peace of God that passes all understandings will preserve our hearts and minds through Christ our Lord with Holy his powerful spirit. Blessed be the Lord God Almighty, he reigns forever.

Religions are devisively devised, implicated and maintained in accordance with the bible by the evil adversary satan. In the bible it refers to God as being a ghost. Most of their relegious retuals are done in the name of the father, son and holy ghost, thats disrespectful. God consist of three components, father Jehovah, Christ his son and Holy his spirit all three combined as one known as the trinity.

A ghost is an evil spirit of a deceased human and a possession of the evil adversary. From a spiritual prospective here's a delusion in reference to Jesus our saviour. It's specified in the bible that in the beginning meaning when the clock started ticking was the word and the word was God. It said that eventually the word became flesh meaning a human and dwell on this earth. That is an dilusion as the true word is Christ, oh what a difference one letter can make, I hope you see it.

Grace is a process that God utilize to accomplish his will, he does not distribute it as a gift to us. God in three dimensions exist in the secret place of the most high inside the realms of glory, not in heaven. We cannot give him glory as a present as it's already his domain. God is omnipotent, omnipresent, perfect and have no beginning or end. We as his people must let our lights shine in good deeds so the world will see and join us in expanding God's kingdom called paradise on the new earth when the fire cools off as it is in heaven.

Let us all give honour and praise to the Lord with all our being and all that is within us as he is holy and worthy of our praises. I will say I enormously appreciate your presence in this venture, It's not my intent to overwhelm you with the substance of it. All the information I share with you here originated from inspirations that impact my mind in meditation. I can assure you that the promises of God are sure, it's been documented that if we meditate day and night we will be like a tree planted by rivers of water that brings fruit in it's season.

We must stand on Christ the solid rock as all other ground are like sinking sand, may our hopes be built on nothing else. We trust in the Lord and know he will not let our trust go in vein, he sent Jesus to rescue us from distruction. We will sing songs of praises to God and utter Holy, holy, holy Lord God almighty as heaven and earth is full of his magnificience and blessings. It's of vital importance that we aspire establishing a personal relationship with our God.

The only way we can approach the throne of grace to communicate with the father and executive is by Christ the only way, not in the name of Jesus. The emphasis that religions put on Jesus belongs to Christ, Jesus was an instrument used by God to redeem humanity of sins and cleanse them of unrightousness both inherited and commited primarily. We must show respect and give thanks and praise to Jesus our saviour for rescueing us. Insist on getting to know the truth and be realesed from religous bondage devised by the evil adversary satan.

Trust in the Lord with your total being and lean not to your own understandings, in all your ways acknowledge him and he will direct your path. Glory to God in the highest, peace and good will to all humanity. The main thing I desire of God and that I seek after with prayers and suplications. To dwell in eternal paradise with Christ and his representative Jesus empowered by Holy his spirit. As humans we operate in polarity like a battery positive and negative.

Our being is positive in Christ while the negative is the evil adversary and his forces in competition for our souls. The product of this combination is called emotions and if not put under control will liquidate and become tears. There are tears of joy from the heart and tears of sorrow from the mind. It's of vital importance not to allow anything to disturb our peace and deprive us of our peace and happiness.

The calender specifies a week to contain seven days, but in our minds there are only three, yesterday, today and tomorrow. Yesterday is in the past and tomorrow is promised to no one. Today is a day that God gave us, we must rejoice and be glad in it. We are presently living in a age when sin is rampant. It's been anounced recently and finally by the head of the Catholic denomination, that homosexuality is now legal. Our compensation package denoted that the wages of sin is death.

Based on my discoveries concerning our final destination if we choose the correct one, paradise will not be as congested as was anticipated. May goodness and mercies be with us all the days of our lives with Christ as our comforter. Based on my exploration of the bible, known as the word of God. I found out that it contain much words from God, uttered and documented by his annointed people even before Jesus was born. Most importantly it's the most comprehensive records of history from before the beginning.

Life is not a game but I will imply that no musical instrument can make a sound without a player. The true Lord/God is Christ a member of the trinity, Jesus is his decendant, representative and instrument of his peace and will. The main comodity religions use in their industry to please the evil adversary is Jesus's name, presenting him as a white cocasion male. In the bible the name of Christ is attached to Jesus making him a surname of Jesus.

Jesus is our messiah, savaior, redeemed, king of the jews and the only begotten/ adopted son of the father. Jesus is totally credible to accept our honor, thanksgiving and praises for rescueing us from distruction. When Jesus was here on earth as human doing the will of the father, Christ spoke through him saying "I'm the resurrection and the life, no one goes to the father but by me" he's the only way, reserection and life of those that choose to be his possession.

I'm only human here in the USA exercising my rights, the

perpose of my inthorogation is to satisfy my curiosity concerning the source of our existence. I'll assume you'll not mind me sharing my findings with you. I'm calling on all humanity to wake up to reality and seek Christ our Lord while he can be found and call upon him while he's near. There will come a time when the sun will no longer shine by day or the moon by night, the earth will stop turning and the clock stop ticking.

As it was in the beginning so it will be in the end, all darkness will turn into light. Presently at this moment in time there is a worldwide health scare as a devised population explosion curtailment process got out of control. I will declear that I'm a child of God and a sheep of his pasture, his promises are sure and I try to emulate his footsteps by making my commitments credible. May the words of my mouth and the medetations of my heart be acceptable to God, as he is my refuge and strength.

Earlier in this venture I did disclose that religions were devised and implemented by the evil adversary satan, as an industry that's designed to accumulate wealth from humans with a vulnorable mentality due to a lack of knowledge. It was predicted that without knowledge people will perish, we are there at this moment in time. The agents that satan appointed are abusing the system by robbing the store houses in enormous propotions of the tithes and offerings people donate to do the work of God.

The most popular ones that's seen on the electronic media travel in their own private jetplanes and live in huge mansions while there are people homeless living on the streets. There are laws of God known as commandments, laws of man and laws of nature, all working together for the benefit of our being as long as we abide by them. Again I will reiterate that there's only on true Lord/God consisting of three components, Jehovah the father and executive, Christ his son executor and Holy his powerful spirit, they have no beginning or end, that's it.

The first thing God created was the universe consisting of all the planets including heaven and earth. The earth was the only planet that was put in motion on a timer and the clock started ticking. That process is known as the beginning of time, and Jesus was absent from that event as he was born from Mary in time later after that ark landed on dry ground. It's specified in the bible when Jesus was born that an angel made the anouncement that a child was born in the city of David a saviour who is Christ the Lord. Christ the Lord is God, allready existed here as he created all things.

Let the celebration begin, we welcomed our savaior Jesus who came to rescue us from sins and cleanse us from all unrightousness. I'm not a religous pastor, priest, minister, prophet, evangelist, pope or even a deacon. I'm just a curious human that made the decision to inthorogate and research the source of our existence. I'ts also my intent to share my findings with the entire english world. I anticipate that sometime in the future God will provide me with the resource required to transulate the contents of my publications in different languages to benifit humanity.

I will disclose that I'm located in the USA and the first place I started this endeavor was the King James version of the bible. Based on my exploration of the bible known as the word of God, I find it to contain words from God instead. God is a spirit and does not utter we have the previlage to interact with him in three dimensions. All directives and utterances and documentations are done by his chosen people even before Jesus was born. The bible is the most comprehensive record of history from before the beginning.

I did encounter numerous inconsistencies in the process of reading it. There are enough evidence to verify my deserned assertions that the contributers that compiled the contents of it included their personal opinions. Most importantly there is no comprehensive alternative to resort to in terms of directives to living a meaningful life, in anticipation of reaching the correct final destination. This project that I'm working on does have a intencive nature as there are times when I become amazed in the proof reading of them.

All the religions involved in the industrial complex are devisive although God displays a togetherness nature, each one operate on a different belief system although they all utilize the bible as their manual. There are reports of an harvesting of souls in progress in an eastern reagon of the globe as the message of redemption goes out throughout the world. In another section of the region there are reports of persecution and supression in the worshiping God.

The city of Atlanta is the capatal of the state of Georgia here in the USA, it's known as having the second largest population of homeless people, even mothers with children live on the street. One of the largest religous mega-churches exist there, with a dollar sigh written all over it. The appointed captain of that ship resides in a mansion outside that city that's decorated in the front yard by Bentley and Rolls Royce cars. Recently he made a request to the congregation for funds from the store house where the tithes and offerings are stored to purchase a new aeroplane, and it was granted.

Heaven is a spiritual domain of God and a reflection of glory, the only human being that was trnsformed and assended to heaven was Jesus. My hope of being in paradise with Christ and Jesus his representative is built on nothing less but the redeeming blood of Jesus and my rightousness. Allways insist on making your utterances credible, do not be influenced by evil forces to conceal them as there will be a judgement for our deeds. There's a prediction that I don't anticipate seing happen, and this is it. "without knowledge people will perish".

It's essential to seek it and be rescued, the posts that you are reading here are copyrighted pages of my books. It's beneficial to seek and acquire any of them and meditate on the contents, presently available are "Truly Amazing Grace" there are others in the process of being published. Any sinereo that's lacking of facts and is composed with a high degree of fantasy is not credible. Jesus is our redeemer, saviour and deserve our thanks and praises for his saving blood. Be sure when you praise him it's from your heart and not an act of incompliance.

I will reinterate that Christ the son of God existed before the beginning of time as God a member of the trinity and have no beginning or end. Religions by utilizing the contents of the bible deceivingly in their worship to please the evil one, rearly mention christ's name as the main source and the only way to the throne of grace to the father. As stated in the bible the name Christ is attached to Jesus as a surname, and all emphasis are placed on Jesus instead of Christ.

None of the members of the trinity of God have ever been an human to commit sins and had to be baptized to wash it away. Religions also denotes that our father God is in heaven his spiritual domain although he is omnipresent, he exist in the place of the most high inside the realms of glory and not on planet heaven. I find my exploratation very extencive but benificial and time consuming due to the acts of documenting of my discoveries. I have recently discovered that the most valuable religion in the industry that's using Jesus's name with Christ attached to it and name their members as saints is worth seventy four billion US dollars.

Secondly the next in line is one that prays to mary the mother of Jesus asking her to pray for them now and at the hour of their passing, worth thirty billion US dollars. This all signifies that their store houses are full and running over by the donation of tithes and offerings in the name of doing the works of God. The entertainment industry here in the US is going broke so to follow the money the stars are getting saved by the bell in wealthy religions.

There is a certain dignetory from the west side of town that started a new religion with a large accomodation facility. He's a very creative businessman as he charges members of the congregation a fee to participate in the worshiping of satan in Jesus name. The appointed agent of satan employ preachers to conduct the worshiping procedure. Recently it was publicly displayed on the electronic media that the agent in question was invited to participate in a service at one of the largest mega-churches and was officially introduced to this nation.

I must caution you that you'll encounter incidents of repitition in this endeavor, it's not intentional but is two fold, 1. I'm utilizing it as an adecive to attach vital substance to your minds and 2. I'm utilizing my acts of creativity to penetrate the minds of the deceaved ones among us. To satisfy the curiosity of this world that mortal life exists on no other planet but the earth, space crafts were sent out to verify that reality. Likewise it's been verified that no one have ever seen any of the three spirit in the trinity of God.

Lord is a title of God making it three Lords in the trinity, Lord Jehovah, Christ our Lord and Lord Holy his powerful spirit. God in three spirits blessed holy trinity!. There are earthly Lords in monarchies, places out there. Christ the true son of God is oroginal with no beginning or end. Christ was never created, born or made to be seen, he is our all in all everlasting and eternal. The Lord God is our life and salvation, the strength of our lives we fear no one.

It's essential to make it a routine to devote moments for meditation on the things of God our sustainer. The owner of our breath and the controller of our destiny. Heaven is not a place somewhere out there far up in the skies, it's a planet in the universe adjacent to the earth occupied by the angelic force of God called angels. There is only one heaven, the statement that says "The heavens declear the glory of God and the fermament shows his handy works" is misleading.

Redenption is not a story, it's a reality whereby we were rescued from distruction by the blood of Jesus. Don't allow yourselves to be deceived by the rethorics of false religions, with the promises of going to heaven and walk the streets of glory by and by. you'll be highly compensated for singing redemption songs to God. Continually give thanks and praises to God for his goodness, mercies, guidance and protection. Holy, holy, holy Lord God Almighty, three spirits in one blessed trinity.

Study and comply with the laws of God to be approved and get yourselves prepared to meet Christ/ God AND Jesus his representative. On that day at the head of the line will be the the passed souls in Christ. Those who made the right decision and are still alive will be transformed in the twinkle of an eyes to join them. There will be weeping, wailing and gnashing of teeth by those left behind to fuel the fire with the evil adversary satan. There will be no mansion in the skies.

We'll be in waiting for that fire to cool off to enter the gates of eternal paradise. Oh what a moment of rejoicing that will be, we will sing and shout for victory. The degree of religous indoctrination is much higher than I assumed. The crutial corrective information I'm insisting on delivering to my international audience is being devisively intercepted. The magnitude of the hinderance is crucial but I'll endeavor to be persistent. The message is clear and intensive as it's precisely based on the unity factor.

These are moments when it would seem like the evil adversary is heading for the finish line with the vulnorable ones among us accompanying him. It will be a blessing to hear from someone in an otmost part of the world like England, to acertain that the message is getting out to the divers places of the earth. The basic laws of God are known as his commandments and there's one that specifies that we should work six days and rest on the seventh.

The morning and the evening including the night was the first day with twenty four hours named Sunday, and the seventh day is Saturday. Remember that disobedience was the first sin committed by Eve in the garden of Eden, influenced by satan to bring Cain that committed the second sin called murder. In the current system of things where the evil adversary satan is god in defience to the laws God. Saturday is the most popular day for business more than usual.

There are a few religions that obey that commandment, God specifically said that if we love him we should keep his commandments. The mejority of humanity are committing sin by disobeying God's laws. The degree of religous indoctrination is much higher than I assumed. The crucial corrective information that I'm insisting on delivering to my international audience is being intercepted by evil forces

In order to get to the right destination called paradise instead of heaven we need to do the following.

1. Bypass the religous Jesus's name and approach the throne of grace by the only way Christ enhanced by the power of Holy his spirit.

2. Disconnect Jesus our saviour from Christ our Lord/God as they are two different spirits. Christ the son of God is original, was never created, made or born. Jesus was born in time from the vergin Mary a human and was a son of man. He was used as an instrument to establish the will of God.

3. God is a trinity, three spirits in one and although Jesus our saviour is affiliated with them, he is not a member of the trinity meaning he's not God.

4. There will be no second coming of Jesus as religions teach, because he's already here omnipresently in spirit accumulating souls. He is working with Christ as a representative doing the will of the father preparing the way to paradise, that the kingdom of God will come on earth as it is on heaven.With God all things are possible according to his will, he is a God of sequence and proposed that all things will work together of our good. If at anytime it seem that coincedentally you are at the right place at the wrong time, go to the father in prayers and suplications by way of Christ to request mercy.

I am Noel Grace the author and will declear that I'm not involved in crap dusting, instead I seek means to fertilize the minds of humanity with potent mental substance as nutrients. One of the most potent and valuable component of our being in our mental faculties is FAITH. It's been unconsciously and not deleberately not mentioned here in this endeavor viraly but it caught up with us. it's been documented and deserned that by grace we are saved through faith not by ourselves, it's a gift from God.

Jesus was accompinied and protected all the way by Holy his spirit who utilized his powers to do the will of the father except in the process of his crusifiction. The basic purpose of Jesus being on this earth was to deliver messages from God and perform mericles. The ultimate was to be crucified to pay in full the price for the sins and transgressions that we committed and those we inherited from our ansesters as far back as Eve and Cain.

I was recently confronted by a religous man concerning errors he encountered in my books plus my habbits of repetition. Without any apology I encouraged him to seek wisdom through knowledge from other sources to his benefit. The older I get is the closer I become to my main source, I have made it a continual routine to meditate on the laws of God day and night.

Here I am sharing the fruits compacted with inspirations from the highest powers with my worldwide audience as it's reaping season. I do rely on the promises of God and he promised that my leaves will not weather and whatever I do will prosper. I have deserned that to make God the owner of our souls is much easier than I imagined. There are intricasies in the scriptures for reconceliation to bring us the joy of the Lord to strenghten our hearts.

I will again reinterate. My perception is that religions were devised and implimented by the evil adversary satan to be a industry. It's based on robbing the store houses containing resources to do God's work in preparation for the coming of his kingdom. God is a God of oneness, togetherness, unity, and other combinding factors. Religions are devisive, delusional, misleading and detrimental to the mental faculties of humanity.

The chosen agents of satan known as popes, priests, ministers, evangelists, elders, investers and others always eventually get wealthy. Because they did'nt acquire wisdom concerning their compensation package, they are lost and is taking innocent beings with them. It's my responsibility to inform them that there will be a day of judgement. From a spiritual perspective I will instigate that there are two thrones available for humanity.

The throne of grace with rewards and the white throne that is detrimental, pick your choice now before it's too late. I must disclose to my worldwide audience that I was given an assignment to accomplish the act of delivering one message. It does take all kinds of people to make the world that involves different languages color and creed. Based on that I have no choice than to utilize the process of repitition. I will incooperate my creativity and eloquence to reach an effective goal. I am appealing to all the masses to engage their capabilities of desernment to see the light to the right pathway.

At this point in the acquisition of inspirations I will wish the entire world peace and good will. It's inconcequential to give glory to God in the highest as it's already his domain and he exist there eternally. Glory is not a credential, it's an eternal domain where God sits on his throne in the beauty of holiness. Oh taste and see that the Lord is good and his mercies endures forever.

I must reveal that I'm having confrontations from religous officials in high positions in that industry. We the people of the world are entitled to our opinions and the philosophies we develop from substantial facts. Based on my experiences in life I made the decision to research the source of our existence and the proper destination for our souls. There is a devised route of deception that's been constructed and in place as an industry called religion.

This business was devised and implimented by the evil adversary satan on a financial infrastructure. There have been a tremendous amount of damage done to the mortal minds of the world. The most critical concern I have is that satan have the capability of accessing our minds even in our sleep with dreams. Another critical issue is that the bible known as the word of God, that I have discovered to contain some words from God.

The bible is highly opinionated by the contributers that wrote it and is being utilized to substantiate the religous industry. I will instigate that you desire to be liberated from the web of evil powers and attain security in the hands of the almighty. In the natural, time is of the essence so the clock keeps ticking. Before we proceed I will inform you that God operates on a template outside of time.

Time is temporary and will eventually burn out but God is

A VISIONARY MESSENGER

eternal with no beginning or end. Our hope is the substance of our anticipation, be sure that your hope is built on nothing less than the blood of Jesus and your rightousness. We as humans are all different in nature, preferences, beleafs and opinions. No man is an island that selfisly stand alone waiting to be submerged, we all need a brother and a chosen friend.

There will always be moments of leisure to treasure, it's more benificial to have a dialogue than a competition. Let your words be disbursed in confedence as your secret is safe with me. Soft words have been spoken and hearts have been broken, always be caring enough to mend a broken heart when it's time for healing. We are all in this endeavor called life together and it's of vital importance that we be there for eachother in times of need.

The world of humanity occupies the planet earth, Jesus our saviour is omnipresently operating on both the earth and heaven doing the will of the father. His primary focus is on the acquisition and accumulation of the submitted souls, the ones that already passed are secured in Christ. Jesus is making preparation for admitting them in paradise where we will be also with Christ. At that moment in time we the ones who choose to be their possession will be transformed in the twinkle of an eye to join them.

Jesus is a decendant and representative of Christ who is a member of the trinity of God but Jesus is not a member. Christ and Jesus are two seperate spirits and I will remind you again and again. I'm appealing to my international audience to seek and acquire my books because they consist of substantial amount of vital information. Most of it was attained through inspirations I acquire while I meditate.

The contents of my publications are potent implications containing mental nutrients for conscious minds. "Truly amazing Grace" is presently available and two others are in the process of being published. I am appealing to the world who are prisioners of religous indoctrinations to seek refuge. Christ is the only way to the throne of grace before the father with our prayers and suplications, not in Jesus name. There need to be more emphasis on Christ our Lord, let us begin to exhault him on high.

Here's an assignment for you, be observant of the reality that the name of Christ is rearly mentioned in churches without it being attached to Jesus as a surname. It's now time to wake up and desern our unrightousness and ask God for cleansing us with the redeeming blood of Jesus. There will come that moment in time when every knee will bow and every toung confess that Christ the son of God a member of the trinity is Lord to please the Almighty.

It's highly benificial to do whatever it takes to acquire the present from God of eternal life, as his kingdom will eventually com on the new earth called paradise as it is in heaven. Because of the false hope that religions have implant inside the minds of the present world, everyone aspire going to heaven and walk the streets of glory. Heaven is a spiritual kingdom of God and the earth will be cleaned by fire to be similar, so whoever made the right choice to be there with Christ and Jesus.

Why would anyone in their right mind aspire going to the present heaven if there will be a new one hear on the cleansed earth called paradise. Vegetation does thrive in water so that's why we still have all that luxury of nature, but based on the next cleansing to be by fire I assume that the new one will be barren. I assume that since we all who get there will be invisible spirits, no one will be identifyable. Oh what a day of rejoising that will be when we get there, we will sing and shout for victory spiritually.

I'm appealing to the world who are prisoners of religions to seek refuge. Christ is the only way to approach the throne of grace before the father with our prayers ans suplications, not in Jesus name. We the world need to put more emphasis on Christ our Lord and exault his name on high. Here's an assignment for you, be observant of the reality of it. The name of Christ is rearely mentioned in churches without being attached to Jesus as a surname.

It's now time to wake up and desern our unrightousness and ask God to cleanse us with the redeeming blood of Jesus. God is the owner of the breath that we breathe and the controller of our destiny, yet fools say in there heart there is no God. The main commodity that religions market is the name of Jesus our messiah, saviour, redeemer, King of the jews and our rescue in times of need.

There places of worship are decorated with a large image of a cocasion male and a cross. In my research I discovered that Mary the mother of Jesus was brown skinned with curly hair. At this moment in time it's insignificant to debate his nationality as he represents all humanity in this world. I'm guilty of repitition but I'll reinterate that religions were devised and implimented by the evil adversary as an industry.

The religious industry was constructed like a vacuum on a financial infrastructure. The agents that satan chose and gave different titles specilize on robbing the storehouses of the tythes and offerings that people donated to do God's works. Most of them become wealthy and is not aware or disregard the promise that they will have to pay a penalty for their actions. Satan is a lier and thief that totally disreguard the commandments of God.

The wages of sin is death and the gift of God is eternal life, as time go bye in the persuit of my life I realize the magnitude of deceived people out there.

THE ULTIMATUM

S ince I've kept you so bored for the duration for consuming the contents of this dialogue, its time to get to the root of things. Recently because I'm doing my research as part of this project I've been listening to some evangelists and what I'm hearing from them are promises to go to heaven through Jesus and at the end of their prayer they say in Jesus name. I saved the best for last for you.

If I had written this valuable substance anywhere in the beginning of this book you would not be hare with me now. Here we go and please do not hold it against me, I'm just a messinger delivering directives as I received them.The main source of my research is the bible and several times I found myself in a state of confusion and had to seek information from other sources.

In my research I found the mention of a female named Lilleth and the concern was about her wisdom then nothing more about her again. After Cain killed his brother Able and ran off to the land of Nod and found himself a wife. It's assumed that Lucifer did the same thing to Lilleth as he did to Eve so Cain's wife was her decendant. Jesus spent extensive amount of time on this earth and disclosed his identity.

The only part of his presence that was not recorded in the history book the bible was his childhood. He chose twelve deciples to work with him doing magficient things like healing and guidelines to follow to expanding the kingdom of the father. Jesus disclosed that it was his father that sent him here for his will to be done. He suffered and died like a lamb to the slaughter and when he arose from the grave he was transformed to being a spirit and assended to heaven.

Presently the name of the son of God and our Lord the third portion of the trinity is Christ. He is the spirit, truth, the Lord, the way, the word and life our all in all. Whenever we pray to the father we should go by way of Christ and not in Jesus or Mary's name. Jesus was an instrument used by God to accomplish a mission, he did what he was sent here to do and moved on to the next stage.

Christ is a spirit, he is Lord and light to our pathway to our father, he is magnificient and emeasurable. If you are observant you'll see that the adversary is rearly mentioned here much as we will not promote him and his agenda but he is in the equation. The name of Lucifer have been changed several times as he is a copycat, it changed to the devil and presently satan.

From my seat in the pavillion of this world I can desern that based on the misleading of the religous leaders the greater portion of humanity will be claimed by satan bound for total distruction in the name of Jesus and that cross. If you are observant you'll see that the emblem of the cross is on all places of worship except for satan worshipers. All three components of the trinity played their part in setting up the kingdom.

In order for us to enter the kingdom of God we must be born again by the spirit and be submurged in water that signifies Jesuse's blood. That procedure must be done in the names of the father Jehovah, his son Christ and Holy his spirit.When we pray our intent is to approach our father and it requires a key to approach the throne of grace and the key is Christ he is spirit and truth.

Most of the religious leaders are leading masses of humanity down the wrong pathway to be claimed by satan destined for total destruction in the name of Jesus. They are giving them the false hope of going to heaven, no human have ever or will ever go to heaven dead or alive. Heaven is an holy planet, residence of the angelic forces of God.

Almighty God Jehovah exist outside of time, the universe he created and utilize the power of his Holy spirit to do his will umnipotently, he is omnipresent also. Heaven was created along with all the other planets including the earth.Those religious leaders need to realize that there will be a penalty to pay for misleading God's people by diverting them in the hands of the adversary the evil one.

Most people beleave heaven is in the skies, thats false. This is a warning to all the world to be very careful and seek to find the right way to paradise on the cleansed earth. Recently I saw an article where someone hope that there was telephones in heaven so they could talk to there family and friends that passed and are now in heaven, this is all a delosion promoted by religions.

The bible is the main source we all rely on for spiritual directives and guidance. It's not my intent for this book to be an alternative but to serve as an awakening to identify the false indoctrinations improvised by the evil adversary using the name of Jesus. There's no where in the bible where Jesus said that he was God and presently people are worshiping him as such, praying in his name,

He requested that we all beleave in God and beleave also in him meaning he is seperate. In the english language the word ALSO is a conjunction that implicate two defferent objects. The bible is classified as the word of God and the holy book, but in my researches I find it to be a credible book containing words from God in terms of his laws, directives and all of his other charactaristics.

There are numerous inconsistencies, for example, east, west, north, south and all in between are directions. The earth is a globe meaning totally round and it's stated in the bible that the earth has four corners. The earth rotates and the sequence of it changes periodically. We must accept Jesus as our savior and redeemer in our hearts, get submerged under water in the name of the father son and Holy his spirit.

Once we do that Holy the spirit take up residence within us like a spiritual GPS to guide us all the way. It's essential that we establish a personal relationship with our father in order to communicate with him by way of Christ. Oh taste and see that the Lord is good and his goodness and mercies endure forever. The Lord is our refuge and strength, we must seek him while he can be found.

The religous preachers keep preaching that Jesus is coming back soon, that will never happen he did his part and was acredited. Do not pray to him or in his name, concentrate on Christ he is our all in all, lilly of the valley and as bright as a morning star. On Christ the solid rock we must stand because all other ground is like sinking sand.

There will be times when we have mountains to climb and rivers to cross overlooking the valleys of distress, always hold to the hands of God. There will be sickness, sorrow and pain to endure because life is not an easy road to travel. Once we accept Jesus as our saviour we are safe in the hands of God. We all do have an appointment with death but once you are a child of God when we go our souls will go to rest in Christ.

We will await our resurection and judgement to be in paradise, the kingdom prepared for us on the new cleansed earth with Christ and Jesus his representative eternally.

CONCLUSION

Happy birthday, today is the first day of the rest of our lives, we anticipate accomplishing all our aspirations. Jesus an instrument of God payed the ultimate sacrifice for our sins acquired or committed in full. By accepting Jesus as our redeemer and savior, we qualify to access the throne of grace to worship Almighty God Jehovah by way of Christ. Let us all give him honor, thanks and praise. Hallilujah.

I appreciate the time you spent exploring my thoughts and inspirations based on what you have been exposed to in this publication. Be sure you do what is required so when your name is called you are there to answer. May peace and love abide and you have a wonderful life and continue to enjoy it's privileges to the fullest.

I hope the revelation of the substance derived from this venture is beneficial to your mind. In the writing of this book I purposely avoided the promotion of satan, that does not mean he is not a force in the equation. That evil force is strong and exist in high places to affect our normal means of existence. There are opposites in all phases of life endeavors, both positive and negative, good and bad, spiritual and evil, right and wrong.

Because of the complex nature of humanity, regardless of the advantage or disadvantage there is someone to participate for the experience. In the world system there will be wars rumors of wars and the operations require weaponry to promote it. After doing a review of the products of my mind, I am convinced that God is utilizing the instruments of my intellect like he did to Solomon. The only thing is that I'm unable to sing the songs of Solomon.

It was predicted a long time ago that without knowledge people will perish, so it's of vital importance that we all seek and acquire and utilize it to the maximum. This publication is designed and meant to be a reference manual in your life process, so the contents can be analyzed by your brain. Based on that concept it's my responsibility to substantiate it with potent contents.

Our imaginations should be utilized to generate innovations to benefit future generations, instead of vain things. Happiness is a flourishing aspect of living life to the fullest, like a flower in bloom. Do not be vulnerable when challenged with adversities in life. Utilize tolerance and listen to your spiritual hearts. The Word, Jesus and Christ are not the same spirit, Christ is who we must concentrate on.

Praying in the name of Jesus is disobeying God's will and that was the first sin committed by Eve. Not much people will go along with me because they are indoctrinated by religions. I will not apologise as this is an asignment I got to share with all the world, the will of God must be done for his kingdom to came on earth as it is in heaven.

I am delighted to make this declaration that I am a son of the true and living God and a sheep of his pasture awaiting the opportunity to go to rest in Christ. I will await my resurection to be awarded my anticipation of inheriting paradise eternally. Hallilujah.

VISIONS FOR OUR MISSION

Noel Grace
Author

Life is a process, the human brain is the processor with the senses as probes to supply a magnitude of the substance to be processed. Repetition is tolerable to promote mental retention, if you are observant you'll see me useing the name Jehovah our God a lot as he is our sustainer. I will confess that I enjoyed the time I invested in doing this publication.

Blessed are the ones that walk not in the council of the ungodly nor stand in the ways of sinners but delight in doing the will of God. They will prosper like trees planted by rivers of water that bring fruit in it's season and whatever they do will prosper. We must forever give thanks and praise to Almighty God by the only way, our intersessor who is Christ the Lord our life and salvation.

Although being invisible spirits in the next realm my hope is that we'll encounter eachother again.

Printed in the United States
By Bookmasters